REMOVING YOUR ROADBLOCKS

TO LOVE, HAPPINESS AND SUCCESS

BY

JAN FORD MUSTIN, PH.D
CLINICAL PSYCHOLOGIST

REMOVING YOUR ROADBLOCKS

Cover Design by Mike Nielsen of Paragon Printing

ISBN 0-9642476-0-7   Paperback

Website address: www.mustin.com

First printing

DEDICATION

This book is dedicated to my parents, Clothille J. Harris and Shelby Jack Harris who have taught me the truth of the famous saying, "Who we are is God's gift to us and who we become is our gift to God."

REMOVING YOUR ROADBLOCKS

REMOVING YOUR ROADBLOCKS

TO LOVE, HAPPINESS AND SUCCESS

TABLE OF CONTENTS

REMOVING YOUR ROADBLOCKS

FOREWORD

by

Ted L. Edwards, Jr., M.D.

Society always seeks conformity, which leads to lives of quiet desperation. People who overcome roadblocks and break the societal bonds that inhibit their personhood are the ones who are able to experience growth, love, happiness and success. This book is about those bonds (roadblocks) and the steps and attitudes required to overcome them. I especially enjoyed *Roadblocks* because it is written in a poignant style with a serious message using the author as an example. She has had to overcome each of these roadblocks herself.

Several years ago in the midst of a lot of personal growth myself, I gave a speech at a local church entitled "Life – A Spiritual Journey in a Physical Body". It is my belief that many of the problems of our physical bodies are brought on by not dealing appropriately with both the obstacles that are placed before us as well as by the lifestyles we choose. Many times a more spiritual approach to life, emanating from a strong spiritual basis within, allows us to deal with external forces more successfully.

Dr. Jan Ford Mustin speaks in this book of dealing with roadblocks so that the spiritual basis within allows us to cope more effectively with the external stresses. These external forces such as financial success, overworking, sex, drugs, alcohol, and various others can all be very tempting as we try to deal with the world by acquiring and having the external forces rule our lives. It is only when we are seeking peace that we begin to look inside ourselves. Dr. Mustin repeatedly comments on the need to remove old ideas, blame, false limitations, and other roadblocks in order to open ourselves for God to work within us. Her concept of God is all encompassing, so this book may fit any religion. There are no limitations here!

I believe that many of us in the healing professions enter them to do our own healing, unconsciously setting up situations that allow us to struggle with our own growth. As I read *Roadblocks,* I was reminded of my own struggles to overcome each of these obstacles over twenty plus years of intense personal growth. Early in our marriage, my wife, Anita, and I made the commitment to each other not to blame. We learned that each of us has to look at conflict between us as either a mirror reflecting something we did not like about ourselves or a trigger to an old, unhealed memory or trauma. My experiences so far are that the obstacles to growth may return in different ways, but once overcome the first time they are easier to recognize and resolve when they occur again.

It is important to note that removing roadblocks is but one facet, albeit a critical facet, to a healthy life. Dr. Mustin also eats a healthy diet, takes nutritional supplements and exercises regularly. She takes time for spiritual growth as well.

As a physician in a conventional-alternative practice, I try to bring out the real area of distress in my patients as I deal with the immediate problem for which they see me. There are many illnesses that reflect deeper unhealed emotional problems, and in my opinion, the healing is more permanent when the underlying emotional issues are removed, allowing the individual to participate in a truly active, healthy life.

Indeed, this is not a book to be read lightly; rather, *Roadblocks* is to be studied, contemplated and acted upon to really effect change and growth towards love, happiness, and success. It takes time and enthusiasm. After twenty years, I am still in the process.

Ted L. Edwards, Jr., M.D.
hello@poweraging.com
Austin, Texas

REMOVING YOUR ROADBLOCKS

REMOVING YOUR ROADBLOCKS

TO LOVE, HAPPINESS AND SUCCESS

INTRODUCTION

Through the years as a clinical psychologist in private practice, I have observed the personal growth and development of thousands of individuals seeking to break through painful periods in their lives, reach their goals, and live rich, fulfilling and meaningful lives. I have been drawn again and again to the simple phrase, "REMOVING YOUR ROADBLOCKS" as a model with universal appeal, application, and value. Several years ago I presented a two-part presentation to a live audience entitled, "REMOVING YOUR ROADBLOCKS" which was televised and also published as an audiocassette album. The public response to this lighthearted but practical offering was surprisingly positive and I have found myself responding to individual requests for copies of quotations, poems, illustrations and anecdotes from this "ROADBLOCKS" model piecemeal by making photocopies of various parts of the presentation, and mailing and faxing them to people committed to positive change and seeking direction and inspiration.

Quite frankly, this form of dissemination of information via Xerox instead of through a publisher was an illustration of my own personal ROADBLOCKS, my procrastination as an author, born of perfectionism, excuses that I was entirely too dedicated to my clinical practice and the needs of my family to commit to the creative process of this book. On the bright side, this period of procrastination has served as a research and development stage, if you will, in my understanding of ROADBLOCKS in the most personal and humbling way possible. You will find within the covers of this book never advice from an expert, but guideposts left by fellow travelers—never "words from the wise" but rather a glimpse of the barriers that block the path of all spiritual beings traveling down life's highway.

I find it both humorous and humbling that my own professional codependency and a strange version of self-importance helped me disguise from myself my fear of the written word. They say that a codependent suffers from a "Vitamin 'E' Deficiency," and experiences "the need to be Everything to Everybody, Everytime!" I had such a deficiency. Each time I approached this book project I experienced a palpable horror at the prospect of being judged by the reader, and imagined being compared to the world's great authors that I studied as an English major and in my graduate studies at N.Y.U. and the University of Madrid. Somehow my reverence for the world's great literatures dating to my liberal arts education had backfired so that I excluded myself from the hallowed written page, like a shabbily dressed child from a sanctuary. In typical ROADBLOCKS fashion, I was comparing this project to writing the proverbial "Great American Novel" and shrinking from the sheer enormity of the literary El Capitan I had erected in my own mind.

My early conditioning to excel scholastically had the unfortunate hangover effect of hindering any publishing aspirations I might have had. I remember this feeling of having so much to say and feeling too inadequate and unworthy to write it down. Long before I had heard the famous parapharse of Biblical Scripture, "From those to whom much is given, much is required," I made it patently clear how it felt to be blessed by good fortune, yet incapable of giving thanks in a tortured poem entitled "Sonnet." Just listen to the self-effacing and self-defeating thoughts I had about myself at the age of nineteen captured in its closing couplet:

> *A reverent fool whose hymns are heresy,*
> *A mouthpiece mute in God's ventriloquy.*

Somehow I suffered from a kind of unenlightened arrogance that was actually a form of pessimistic egotism, a kind of terminal uniqueness that fueled my poetry and my fondness for the metaphysical poets. Strangely, the bond I felt for the likes of Alexander Pope and John Donne led me at first into graduate studies in literature, and towards a career as a professor of comparative literatures. But it was the softer stories of women I met in Spain, stories of their unlived dreams, their frustrations, their hopes and their passions that led me down a different life path. I felt strongly pulled into the traffic of real lives and away from the rigors of academia, absolutes and abstraction.

Is there any wonder that it has taken more years than I'll admit to finally record my thoughts in the form of a book? Since then, thankfully, my sense of gratitude for what I have learned about myself and my profound respect for the thousands of teachers I have had as clients have helped me overcome the perfectionism so evident in my poem written at age nineteen. Since then, I've learned that the vicissitudes of life mostly seem haphazard and inelegant, but that woven through them there is a simplicity of spirit that connects us all and smoothes out the imperfections of our life scripts.

I believe it is true that, all in all, life is a pretty good therapist, and I'm counting on its corollary truth, that life is a pretty good editor too.

Meanwhile, my self-imposed barriers to self-expression seemed limited to the world of publishing and, from the weekly speaking engagements from what I like to refer to as my "Church Lady Era," (during which I overcame knocking knees and the cotton mouth of stage fright to dutifully deliver weekly Sunday morning announcements), I finally emerged (despite myself) to become a fairly accomplished public speaker and, only then, began to enjoy immensely the creative process of blending poetry and prose, pathos and humor into a variety of entertaining presentations. I called on my background in literature and my love of story telling to provide personal and human punctuations for my talks. To my delight, my audiences seemed instantly mesmerized by the stories and poetry embedded in my talks, clamoring for copies of rhymes and verses to add to their own personal collections. The power of poetry helped them relate to the heavier and more challenging aspects of my message, helped open up their hearts and minds and perhaps helped make more palatable the presentation of the often-bittersweet truths of our human condition.

The fun of sharing my insights as a therapist through speaking became even more so when I began to play with staging each talk as a production, replete with music, stage props and lots of visual humor, and even letting it all go over the airwaves on radio and television, knowing that it was possibly helping thousands of people as well as providing me with a creative outlet for what I hoped was meaningful work beyond my role as a clinical psychologist.

I used to love writing scripts for my daily radio program entitled, "The Success Connection" in which I offered inspirational thoughts for the day, embedded in humorous anecdotes and tall tales. Being a conduit for lessons learned was actually a lot of fun, and I relished the time I spent each week writing magazine and other periodical articles for mostly local distribution. No matter how unbounded my enthusiasm for writing, somehow I shrank from the spotlight that I associated with writing an actual book. I share this with the reader as a kind of credential, which helps qualify me as an expert on the subject of this work— ROADBLOCKS. I understand very well the feeling of being less than I can be. I know first hand the painful knowledge that I have frequently held myself back, and not dared to move ahead. In short, I understand ROADBLOCKS from the inside out.

Hopefully this personal disclosure, this crossing of the proscenium arch on the part of the author, has served to illustrate that even those of us whose life's work it is to help others remove ROADBLOCKS have our own internal struggles. In fact, it is quite probable that many if not most psychiatrists and psychologists were drawn to the helping profession mostly out of a deeply personal yearning to "get it right," to figure out the way people work, and thereby to heal ourselves.

I have yet to meet the individual who has not run headlong into his or her own ROADBLOCKS and often not even recognized the fact. Curiously, often it is when we are spinning our wheels in high gear, stopped in our tracks by a series of ROADBLOCKS and feeling terribly alone and ashamed about our predicament, that we do not recognize that we are in a kind of global traffic jam, or even cosmic pile up, if you will. None of us is actually as terminally unique as we perceive ourselves to be, whether in our sense of superiority or inferiority. ROADBLOCKS lie in the path to fulfillment, understanding and wisdom for us all.

I realize full well that in employing an acronym such as "ROADBLOCKS" as the mnemonic backbone for this book I am surrendering any pretense of erudition or possibility of original thought to everyday formulaic practicality. After all, I *am* a practitioner, working by appointments, hour-by-hour, and day-by-day with people who seek professional help at critical times in their lives. They come to me and my colleagues to discover for themselves how to make their lives more meaningful, how to make them work. This decision as a clinician to do what works in helping people as opposed to pursuing a career of academic research, professional journal articles and collegial acceptance and recognition is one that I made a long time ago. So, risking the stigma of this book's being labeled as "pop psychology" or "self-help literature" is really nothing new for me. I have stalled long enough behind my own ROADBLOCKS to let the risk of seeming like the red-haired stepchild of "serious-minded research" hold me back any longer. I am quite ready to move ahead with the trip.

Along this line, being a little out of step, a bit of a maverick in my field, is actually becoming familiar. Often, when I am invited to speak to various groups I like to introduce myself by reminding the audience that, it is commonly believed that the practice of psychology is nothing more than "the care of Id by the odd." This usually brings a ripple of appreciative chuckles and leads us right into a real-world, real-time, exchange, and we all have fun and learn some about our foibles and what it takes to become self-aware and begin to gain mastery over various aspects of our lives that are puzzling to us. So, as I begin to share with you this ROADBLOCKS model that I've had such fun with on platforms and on people's TV sets, I am reminded of the great quote by Marianne Williamson and used in his inaugural address by Nelson Mandela of South Africa:

Our deepest fear is not that we are inadequate.
Our deepest fear is that we are powerful beyond measure.
It is our light, not our darkness that most frightens us.
We ask ourselves, who am I to be brilliant, gorgeous, talented and fabulous?
Actually, who are you not to be?

Your playing small doesn't serve the world. There's nothing enlightened about shrinking so that other people won't feel insecure around you.
We are born to make manifest the glory of God that is within us. It is not just in some of us; it's in everyone.

And as we let our own light shine, we unconsciously give other people permission to do the same.
As we are liberated from our own fear, our presence automatically liberates others.

Removing our ROADBLOCKS requires personal courage and commitment. Thankfully, through the mere recognition of the *nature* of our various ROADBLOCKS we gain the perspective and awareness that assist us automatically with the removal of those ROADBLOCKS. Clearly, it is true that knowledge is power, and empowered with greater self-knowledge, we are able to begin to remove our personal ROADBLOCKS and clear the way to our goals. As a wise friend once told me, "Awareness is a dangerous thing. Once you have gained it, you can never go back!"

This book is devoted to the process of assisting each of us in the renewal of our awareness of our own personal

ROADBLOCKS, and through awareness, the empowerment to remove them. We will find that, while our respective roads in life may diverge, the ROADBLOCKS we face are as universal and as recurrent as are the emotions we experience in our struggles to move on, accomplish our dreams and become all that we dream we can be. ROADBLOCKS are a natural part of the journey. They help us grow in character and develop greater wisdom, perspective and compassion for others.

This book is designed to help provide you with practical tools of recognition, the self-acceptance to see the obvious, and then, with greater perspective, to see beyond apparent obstacles and free yourselves of undue frustration, confusion and delay. It is intended to assist in your very personal journey of self-awareness and personal development in order that you relish the journey towards your hopes and dreams. It is offered with all humility from one traveler to another, as each of us is guided by those ahead and is expected to assist those just behind us on the path.

The removal of one's ROADBLOCKS creates a clear and open road, a new path to travel freely through our lives. Removing our own personal ROADBLOCKS also clears the way for those who follow our lead, those for whom we unwittingly set an example. Removing our ROADBLOCKS is a personal transformational journey, not a race, but an inside job. Removing our ROADBLOCKS is a process of daily, moment-to-moment choices to perfect ourselves in order to move spiritually towards our own destinies.

To all of you embarking upon this journey, committed to the process of exploring yourself and becoming more than you ever thought you could be, I say, "Welcome!" It is my hope that this book will draw you in with the power of the stories of actual people's lives, and the truth that is stranger than fiction. Illustrations in both prose and poetry have been selected very carefully, as we are most often led by our hearts, and only later use our cognitive skills to rationalize our emotional choices. In the words of Stanley Kunitz, the tenth poet laureate of the United States, "Poetry is the medium of choice for giving our most hidden self a voice—the voice behind the mask that all of us wear. Poetry says, 'You are not alone in the world: All your fears, anxieties, hopes, despairs are the common property of the race.'"

You will surely find this a great personal adventure that will take you places you never even imagined. The process will, at times, be challenging, humbling, possibly even frightening, but the rewards in human compassion and a sense of mission, purpose and belonging in the universe are beyond price.

In the immortal words from Robert Frost's *The Road Less Traveled,*

> *I shall be telling this with a sigh*
> *Somewhere ages and ages hence,*
> *Two roads diverged in a wood and I*
> *Took the one less traveled by,*
> *And that has made all the difference.*

REMOVING YOUR ROADBLOCKS

REMOVING YOUR ROADBLOCKS
THE JOURNEY BEGINS

 **is for RESISTANCE**

"When everything seems to be going against you, remember that the airplane takes off against the wind, not with it."

Henry Ford

is for "RESISTANCE," the first and possibly most obvious way we stop short of realizing our potential. Some of you are experiencing some RESISTANCE at this very moment, as you consider whether you want to read a book dedicated to helping you transform your lives into the ones you have dreamed of. The simplest way to begin to think of the RESISTANCE to change, to doing something new and different, to beginning a project, is to view RESISTANCE as a response to the natural fear of the unknown. Just as other members of the animal kingdom function according to the "fight or flight" response to perceived threat, so too are we hardwired for this automatic, knee jerk alarm that starts in our reptilian brain. This response of "fight or flight" has been adaptive for millions of years and has allowed us to evolve to our current position in the phylogenetic tree of life. It becomes a ROADBLOCK, however, when we fail to recognize when our "alarm system" is malfunctioning and when our lives and dreams get stuck in a kind of perpetual "false alarm." RESISTANCE becomes a ROADBLOCK when we fail to face our fears thoughtfully and determine if they are real or imagined, actual threats or merely "monsters under the bed."

There are a myriad of adages that assist us in fortifying ourselves against this most common of emotional reactions to the unknown, not the least well known of which is, "The longest journey begins with a single step."

Perhaps you remember the wonderfully zany film from the eighties with Richard Dreyfus and Bill Murray titled, "What

1

About Bob?" in which the psychologist played by Dreyfus had written a self-help book called *Baby Steps* and his patient (played by Murray) was facing his own ROADBLOCKS and taking those baby steps all the way to fame and fortune, while the psychologist was reduced to the pathetic status of psychiatric patient and victim of his own patient's enthusiastic embrace of his own teachings. The film was, for me, hysterical in its dramatization of the fact that RESISTANCE to change is universal, and insanity has no respect for authority, status or station, and makes no distinctions between the rich and the poor. It has absolutely no regard for credentials, ZIP codes, sides of the railroad tracks—in short, insanity takes no prisoners. In a nutshell (pardon the pun), an operational definition of insanity is simply when you keep on doing the same thing and expecting different results, or, more whimsically, "If you always do what you've always done, you'll always get what you've always got."

When we look at RESISTANCE to change, fear of the unknown, from a purely evolutionary perspective, we see that, as with each of the other ROADBLOCKS, it responds to a biological imperative, to assist in survival of the individual and ultimately, the species. Within reason, RESISTANCE to change is an elemental part of homeostasis, a guiding principle inherent in every part of the universe providing stability and order rather than utter cosmic chaos. By approaching the unknown with caution, embarking on a process of information gathering and then, once assured of a high probability of safety and payoff for the risk of venturing beyond our comfort zones, we are in "survival mode" and, like all other animals, more likely to persist past procreation and thereby protect, not only ourselves but our species.

But even the biologist must weigh the survival of the individual with the evolution of the species, which relies too on the element of change, on risk taking, facing fears, and moving forward into the unknown. We know that as a species we have evolved from a much more primitive model of mankind, and in seventh grade many of us memorized the evolutionary axiom, "ontogeny recapitulates phylogeny." As individuals, then, during our brief lifetimes, we must evolve as well, in order to fulfill our personal destiny. While there is a fine balance between playing it safe and being a fool, it seems that this inherent need to take risks and face one's fears is indeed innate, genetically programmed, part of who we are. By nature, each of us is designed to become more than we ever imagined we could be, more than we ever dreamed.

Lloyd C. Douglas really captures the teleological nature of this inborn need we each have to develop, change, face our fears and sail into uncharted waters:

> *We are not drawn from Behind, but lured from Before!*
> *Not pushed, but pulled! Magnetized from Beyond!*

Over the years, I have observed as my clients courageously face their own fears as they begin the process of therapy in order to improve their lives. Just the mere act of voicing the problem, admitting that it exists and that one needs a little help, is, for some, quite a formidable obstacle. By the time I ever see these people for the very first time, most of them have grappled with the ROADBLOCK of RESISTANCE and have been "pulled from beyond" to overcome any feelings of embarrassment or shyness about seeking professional help. The Ethiopian proverb, "We are only as sick as our secrets," is absolutely true, and already, by our first meeting, they have begun to dismantle the ROADBLOCK of RESISTANCE and are well on their way.

Most people, when they begin counseling, are feeling powerfully motivated by painful life circumstances, feelings of loss, grief, and self-rejection or low self-esteem. Many are in a position of unusual vulnerability and insecurity as they enter my office for the first time. They must assess for themselves if they feel safe enough, secured by the atmosphere of my office and staff, to speak with me about the nature of their situation in order even to begin to tackle it together with me as a team. Sometimes the individual's feeling of RESISTANCE is so overwhelming that the initial phone call is never made. Sometimes the phone call is made and there is a last-minute cancellation of the no-charge orientation appointment, designed to help them with overcoming their RESISTANCE by offering information without obligation so that they have more familiarity with the path they are considering to take. Sometimes the client sails right through the initial points of turning back and meets with me rather comfortably, elucidating the nature of the help they seek and making impressive strides towards positive changes, only to draw back later in the process. No matter what stage of what pursuit we may feel a tug of doubt and a feeling of avoidance (like wanting to turn off the alarm clock on a Monday morning and pull the covers back up over our heads), we can begin to recognize RESISTANCE for what it is. To quote a late, great friend of mine, Jack Boland, RESISTANCE is frequently a problem, not only when we are facing the fearsome, but also when "the good becomes the enemy of the better."

RESISTANCE to change is when we have made friends with the status quo. Our comfort zones may no longer be comfortable; in fact, they may be downright excruciating. But, at least they are familiar. RESISTANCE is the dynamic of resigning ourselves to being in a rut, even if it is a problematic, cramped and very muddy rut. There is a sign on the Alaskan-Canadian Highway, the "AlCan," that reads: "Choose your rut carefully—you'll be in it for the next 200 miles." Some of us know first hand exactly how that feels.

RESISTANCE is when we have begun to furnish our own self-created dungeons and prisons and have begun to feel as though "home is where your stuff is." RESISTANCE to change may be when we have emotionally twisted ourselves into pretzels in order to accommodate other people and have gone numb to the pain. Chronic RESISTANCE to change, repeatedly backing away from challenges, can leave us feeling like victims, ready to piggyback on some political message from the media that makes it easy to blame another group for our plight rather than seeing that we ourselves have chosen the victim role by our own inaction and personal cowardice.

To overcome our ROADBLOCK of RESISTANCE we must abandon our comfort zones by setting goals and committing ourselves to them. Of course, achieving goals involves change, and they say the only person who likes change is a wet baby! If we do not set specific goals for ourselves, we will slowly sink into a sea of mediocrity. Zig Ziglar wrote, "You have to be careful not to become a 'wandering generality.' You must strive to become a 'meaningful specific.'"

The great pioneer in psychology, Erik Erikson, once wrote, "All 'graduations' in human development mean the abandonment of a familiar position . . . all growth . . . must come to terms with this fact." And the "Father of Psychology," William James, advised, "Be not afraid of life. Believe that life is worth living and your belief will help create the fact."

RESISTANCE, like addiction, is cunning and baffling and assumes many disguises. Sometimes it is as simple as the universal experience of viewing oneself in a three-way mirror in the swimsuit department. When faced with our mirrored image, many of us are displeased to say the least with the "cellulite" or "love handles" of harsh reality. RESISTANCE is also that nasty feeling of being offended when a friend, relative or even therapist, draws our attention to one of our shortcomings. So conditioned to believing that we must be flawless in order to be loved and have our needs met, that any reminder that we are works in progress seems to threaten our very survival. Typically, we stew over a friend's critical comment about us that holds at least a kernel of truth. We are slow to realize that we can improve only that which we know to be in error. RESISTANCE keeps us from appreciating the constructive criticism that could actually assist us in our course correction, just like the electronic compass on a jetliner. They say that an airplane is off course at least 90 percent of the time and makes literally thousands of course corrections during a flight. If only we could accept the reality that each of us is usually somewhat off course, RESISTANCE would be far less common a ROADBLOCK. If we could swallow our pride as we go down life's highways and stop now and then to ask directions, the trip would surely be smoother, more enjoyable, and we would more likely end up at our desired destinations!

RESISTANCE to change is so common, so everyday, and so indiscernible that it is sometimes easiest to recognize it among isolated and often stereotyped endeavors such as the national preoccupation with losing weight. The following verse by an unknown author about the dilemma shared by millions who suffer RESISTANCE to starting to exercise says it all:

Being the Best

I spent a fortune
On a trampoline,
A stationary bike
And a rowing machine,
Complete with gadgets
To read my pulse,
And gadgets to prove
My progress results
And others to show
The miles I've charted—
But they left off the gadget
To get me started!

It seems that it is a fairly widely held misconception that in order to attempt something new, we must first feel ready to do so. In fact, this belief stems from what I call "emotional reasoning," that is, the feeling that, only once I am really comfortable doing something is it time for me actually to begin. In fact, in reality, the converse is true. "Behavior precedes adjustment" is a well-researched psychological principle showing that it is through the doing of the deed that we break out of our comfort zones into the brave new world, the unfamiliar, and finally stand a chance to achieve greatness. In fact, it was pioneering psychologist William James who wrote,

To feel brave, act as if we were brave, use all our
will to that end, and courage will very likely replace
fear. If we act as if from some better feeling, the
bad feeling soon folds its tent like an Arab and
silently steals away.

RESISTANCE to change has been pondered by all the world's great philosophers and is the subject of innumerable essays and treatises. Emerson advises, "Do the thing and you'll have the power." Eleanor Roosevelt opined, "You must do the thing you think you cannot do." The modern, though ineloquent maxim, "Fake it till you make it" challenges us all to face our RESISTANCE squarely, with bold defiance, just as peoples all over the world respond to the "Swoosh" of Nike and, "Just Do It!"

In my practice, I have been impressed by the depth of angst and the sense of low-grade grief that accompanies unchallenged RESISTANCE in the lives of my clients, as well as by the resultant avoidant lifestyle that they experience when they are not living their dreams. Some state outright that they feel that life is passing them by or that they have "settled" for a "ho-hum" existence. Many represent their feelings as those of loneliness; some identify them as anxiety or depression, and many present with secondary symptoms in the form of problems with substance abuse (whether food, alcohol or other drugs), workaholism, codependency, and a variety of other "isms" or ways to medicate one's feelings. Interestingly, when we do not push past our own issues of RESISTANCE to experience the exhilaration of mastery and feeling alive, we are usually left with feelings of being diminished, feelings of ennui, disappointment, and lethargy— even despair. It's as though each of us has an internal compass of courage and we know, from moment to moment whether we are facing or running away from our personal challenges.

Now, I myself am passionate about sports, both as an amateur player and a fan, but consider, if you will, our national obsession with sports, soap operas and other vicarious spectator phenomena. Ask yourselves the question of how and why millions of us will spend countless hours whipping ourselves up into a frenzy over football, basketball, soccer, and tennis. Ever wonder why we are a nation characterized by obesity, drug and alcohol abuse and premature death from stress-related diseases? It seems that the path of least RESISTANCE from our achievement of personal greatness might just be that of vicarious achievement through one's favorite team, mini-series or even nightly "talking heads" news programs. Without a proactive approach to our own lives, many of us merely default to a drone-like acceptance of socially sanctioned "entertainment" that is processed for the lowest common denominator and has the cultural value of junk mail. Rather than facing our RESISTANCE to pursuing our own personal dreams, we busy ourselves with tailgate parties and Superbowl Sundays. No doubt, RESISTANCE to overcoming fears is universal and our particular culture and economy capitalize on this in grand fashion. Unfortunately, vicarious living has a limited shelf life and questionable nutritional value, ultimately leaving a nation spiritually malnourished, looking to afternoon talk shows for emotional sustenance and spiritual guidance.

It has been my experience that the happiest people I know are not necessarily the wealthiest monetarily, nor are they ones with the best wardrobes or sex-lives. As I have seen clients from every walk of life share their stories from across the room, I have noticed that those engaged in the pursuit of goals worthy of them are feeling truly alive and happy. It is said that there are three kinds of people: "Those who make things happen, those who watch things happen, and those who ask, 'What happened?'"

One of the feelings most prevalent among clients I treat for depression is a vague but nagging sense of regret for risks not taken. These people have felt the feeling of RESISTANCE and have backed away, turning from an opportunity to grow. Author Susan Jeffers writes, "We will always feel the fear as long as we are growing!" People who shrink from this fear, also begin to shrink in their own eyes and begin to feel a sadness that is hard to put into words. It's as though they have stopped living their own lives and, on some level, they know it. This internal awareness of having backed down from greatness registers inside us as feelings of inadequacy, shame, and an emptiness that very few of us ever verbalize. We are simply aware of what "might have been" and we silently and secretly ask ourselves, "What went wrong?" Plagued by a vague sense of dissatisfaction, many of my clients enter therapy asking, "Is that all there is?" hoping to discover that their life can expand to hold the wonders they once envisioned in their youth.

Unhappiness seems to be the shadow of our RESISTANCE to growth and action. Happiness, then, would be its corollary. Tom Peters defines happiness this way: "Happiness has to do with being engaged, being excited in any sense of the word about any task." Leo Buscaglia also describes people in action, freed from their everyday ruts as he writes, "The happiest people love many, many things with a passion," and Franklin D. Roosevelt claimed, "Happiness lies in the joy of achievement and the thrill of creative effort." Allan K. Chalmers really distilled the essence of joy, when he wrote, "The grand essentials of happiness are something to do, something to love and something to hope for."

I am frequently impressed by the public response to media coverage of enormous loss of human life through terrorist acts or natural disasters such as tornadoes, hurricanes, floods and fires. Similarly, I am struck by the powerful public reaction to tragedy involving the premature death of a celebrity, such as President John F. Kennedy or Princess Diana, or to the horrors of the Holocaust of Nazi Germany, the fiery spectacle of the Hindenburg zeppelin or the unspeakable acts of terrorism. What strikes me the most about this phenomenon of our capacity for collective grief is our contrasting lack of awareness and concern for the much more common, premature spiritual and existential deaths of millions, possibly billions of people by virtue of their succumbing to RESISTANCE to change, fear of the unknown, living unlived lives! It's as though we appreciate the sensational and the spectacular events and give them our full and riveted attention, while the subtle sufferings and silent sacrifices elude us. This phenomenon allows the ROADBLOCK of RESISTANCE to be a true silent killer of dreams.

It seems that we respond strongly to the visuals of a nation cast into mourning by an assassin's bullet, the decimation of a village by guerilla attack, the twisted remains of a light plane and the carnage of war, but we do not appreciate the incremental and subtle signs of tragedy all around us. We silently turn away from challenges and opportunities that would allow us to reach our full potential and to feel the exhilaration of personal growth, of mastering ourselves and allowing ourselves to be citizens of the world, to feel expansive and fully alive. There is a lot of truth in the saying that, "Most people, by age 25 are dead already—Just not used up yet." An unknown author says it even better:

Opportunities Missed

There was a very cautious man
Who never laughed or played
He never risked, he never tried,
He never sang or prayed.

And when one day he passed away,
His insurance was denied,
For since he never really lived,
They claimed he never died!

RESISTANCE might be compared with driving down the road of life with one's foot on the brake, looking into the rear view mirror instead of straight ahead. With this driving style you would likely lurch forward and back, side to side, never making any smooth or significant headway. Driving with your foot on the brake you would probably not enjoy the ride, miss the scenery along the way, and at some point begin to wonder what the trip was all about anyway! With RESISTANCE, the would-be driver rejects the role of risk-taker and decision-maker, and assumes the role of passenger, merely watching the world go by. With RESISTANCE, there is an absence of commitment to the road as well as to the adventure of the journey.

Ruth Mason Rice has a clever verse to punctuate this fear of risk-taking:

It's a risk to have a husband
A risk to have a son
A risk to pour your confidence out to anyone
A risk to pick a daisy, for there's sure to be a cop
A risk to go on living—but a greater risk to stop!

It seems like it might be a good idea to include in our required curricula for all children in school courses on the joys of recognizing and removing their RESISTANCE to growth, new opportunities and risk-taking. This could be integrated into their early school years as part of what I term "emotional literacy," a fundamental life skill that will help them throughout their lives with emotional expression and communication in order to live their lives fully, productively and happily.

Along with their "ABC's," arithmetic and computer skills training, children would learn about the most important thing of all, their own emotional dynamics. They would learn to read, not only books, but also themselves and others and learn to master the art of selecting emotional responses and expressing these in a healthy and fully human manner. Emotional literacy would certainly supercede our valuation of reading, writing or arithmetic, and youngsters throughout the world would learn how to live life consciously, rather than reactively. Emotional literacy fosters self-acceptance, mutual respect and understanding among all ages and ethnic groups and helps facilitate peaceful and cooperative relationships among classmates and among nations.

Among the lessons of emotional literacy would be a primer on commitment, the key to removing RESISTANCE from our paths. Understanding that commitment is integral to living powerfully and by choice helps us unlock many a door and remove the ROADBLOCK of RESISTANCE. Perhaps W. H. Murray says it best in his verse:

Commitment

Until one is committed there is hesitancy,
The chance to draw back, always ineffectiveness.
Concerning all acts of initiative (and creation)
There is one elementary truth,
The ignorance of which kills countless
Ideas and splendid plans:
That the moment one definitely commits oneself,
Then Providence moves too.

All sorts of things occur to help one
That would otherwise never have occurred.
A whole stream of events issues from the decision,
Raising in one's favor all manner of unforeseen
Incidents and meetings and material assistance,
Which no man could have dreamed
Would have come his way.

Therefore, the antidote for RESISTANCE is commitment. We learn to replace avoidance with action, fear with faith, and hesitancy with boldness.

In that spirit, let us go forward with this task of REMOVING YOUR ROADBLOCKS, and heed the directive of Goethe who wrote,

Whatever you can do, or dream you can, begin it.
Boldness has genius, power, and magic in it.

"R" is for RESISTANCE

 is for **OLD IDEAS**

"A great many people think they are thinking when they are merely rearranging their prejudices."

William James

is for "OLD IDEAS." Clearly, many old ideas fall into the categories of common sense, traditions, and values, even wisdom. When these theories, concepts and beliefs become a true ROADBLOCK, it is when they no longer hold true, are no longer relevant to our ever-changing reality and when they blind us to the truth and limit our potential. As a ROADBLOCK, OLD IDEAS simply must be identified and hauled out of our path, in order that we might live enriched, meaningful and fulfilling lives.

Sociologists Peter L. Berger and Thomas Luckmann have captured the making of OLD IDEAS as ROADBLOCKS in their brilliant book, *The Social Construction of Reality: A Treatise in the Sociology of Knowledge.* In this perennial masterpiece, they shatter our false illusions and assumptions about reality, by discussing the science of phenomena, or "phenomenology." A fifty dollar word with a fancy Webster definition, phenomenology is "the scientific description of consciousness and its intentional objects, in their pure essences, suspending assertions of their existence independent of consciousness." Phenomenology simply requires us to look carefully at our relationship with our thoughts, assumptions, beliefs, and to challenge what we might otherwise take for granted. For the rest of us real people, phenomenology merely requires us to ask, "Why?" and to take responsibility for being co-creators of our own realities, by becoming conscious of our interpretations, reactions and responses to the world.

Through the process of our social construction of reality,

perceptions and beliefs about reality are accumulated somewhat randomly from our own personal experiences, and learned from observations or teachings of those who went before. This "knowledge" is absorbed from school, television, books and now the Internet and a million other sources. In general, "reality" is a cut-and-paste proposition that we sometimes assume to be universal, actually true, and unchanging. The fact is, many times, our hand-me-down information is imprecise, if not totally incorrect and no longer applicable. This aggregate of impressions, reactions, defense mechanisms and ways of life that we call "culture" arise on the individual level, the family and community level, as well as at the national and global level, and shapes what we accept as our society—even our humanity. Phenomenology has opened our eyes to the process by which this ROADBLOCK of OLD IDEAS is created, and through understanding, we assume our proper position in recreating our world views, our relationships with others, and, most importantly, our understanding of ourselves.

The ROADBLOCK of OLD IDEAS has its origins in our childhood. Let's face it. As children, all of us were looking up at the world. Our perspective early in life was very near the carpet or the sidewalk. From where we stood, when we finally did, our eye level was beneath the kitchen table, the countertops and the windowsill. I remember thinking that my five-year old neighbor John McKinney was Superman because he could reach the doorbell when I could not. As children, our physical size is part and parcel of how we construct the ROADBLOCK of OLD IDEAS. From the time we begin to develop a self-concept, our physical size and capabilities are interwoven into our feelings of inadequacy, dependency and a wish to master our environment. Our earliest feelings as children, the phenomenon of imprinting on very own early memories, become part of our OLD IDEAS separating "us" (children) from "them" (grown-ups).

Often, OLD IDEAS are merely perfectly good concepts and beliefs that we may have outgrown, like the Easter Bunny or the Tooth Fairy. Just because we reinterpret them from an adult perspective, does in no way need to diminish or devalue their original place in our memories or in the way we cherish our childhoods. Identifying OLD IDEAS can be as neutral and productive a process as culling through our closets after a long winter to make room for spring clothing. Identifying OLD IDEAS allows us to move forward into emotional maturity with new and personally selected ideational and spiritual garments, values and beliefs that empower us to live more fully and freely.

We have a term for happenings that are throw backs to an earlier time—"anachronisms." OLD IDEAS are basically leftover beliefs that have outworn their usefulness. Whether they are actually anachronistic or misfits in some other way, OLD IDEAS all too often go unrecognized as such, and become self-defeating or ineffective elements of our individual and collective perception of reality. A very common and elemental example of OLD IDEAS derives from our childhoods when we read fairy tales and accepted the happy ending, "and they all lived happily ever after." As small children, we believed this quite literally, as small children do, and we imprinted on the images of the hero and heroine riding off happily into the sunset. As adults, we sometimes carry this OLD IDEA into our first love, college, marriage, and beyond, much as we might continue to hold onto worn out and childish toys or comic books. The moral of the story is that the adults who believe that the purpose of life is to seek happiness are typically the most unhappy adults. It was Emerson who penned, "The unexamined life is not worth living" and it is equally true that an OLD IDEA unexamined is not worth keeping.

As we mature and learn that happiness is a by-product of a life with purpose and the pursuit and attainment of goals worthy of us, we update our OLD IDEAS and live with higher levels of joy and feelings of connectedness with other people everywhere. We understand that we can and do make a difference on the planet and that the nature of our impression on the earth and on our fellow travelers is a moment-to-moment choice. True joy and fulfillment come to those of us who often forget to think of our own happiness because we are so involved in living our lives on purpose, consciously and with commitment to a higher calling. On an individual basis, each of us has quite a collection of these OLD IDEAS within our thoughts and images that constitute our self-concept, our sense of who we are and what our capabilities might be. Most of us operate our lives under the misconceptions, the "anachronistic" beliefs, that we are limited in our abilities in ways that might have been fairly accurate when we were decades younger, years less experienced than we are today. Our perceptions of ourselves are frequently "stuck" in OLD IDEAS that over time have become habitual ways of self-reference. Illustrating this is quite simple. Consider yourself how you were labeled as a child, teased by siblings or playmates, made to feel diminished or rejected or discouraged by comments or treatment by other people. Early impressions about ourselves tend to resist change and often persist into adulthood despite conflicting evidence to the contrary.

Fairy tales of childhood give way to the fantasies of adolescence. Rites of passage for young adults include fraternity hazing, drunken orgies in the honor of Bacchus, the mythological god of wine, indiscriminate, "recreational" or "casual" sex and other sensual excesses—all socially sanctioned and "all in good fun." Somehow our society and others have turned a collective blind eye to what is often at least a full decade of our youth's indiscretions and have actually encouraged and exploited risky behavior for the sake of commercial gain, if not voyeuristic pleasure. A far cry from the innocuous OLD IDEAS from our childhood (in which we may have bribed Santa with milk and cookies, knowing full well that Mom and Dad were making all that racket assembling the bicycle in the living room), the OLD IDEAS of adult fantasy life may actually be dangerous business. Our Mothers Against Drunk Drivers, our Academy Award Ceremonies dominated by red ribbons to fight against AIDS, and other impassioned crusades to save victims of violence and disease are just one flick of the remote from "Wild on E" and other expose's of "reality television" cashing in on sensationalism. Somehow, we perpetuate the OLD IDEA that fantasy is harmless, even when we are playing with our very lives and those of others. Our cultural self-destructive and addictive behaviors do take victims, all right—not only the individuals who compromise their values and sacrifice their ideals, but those who lose their lives and those whose lives are endangered by the OLD IDEA that "living la vida loca," is simply an integral and harmless part of being happy, and having fun.

If you are wondering how your ROADBLOCK of OLD IDEAS may have detoured you from your dreams, even stopped you from reaching your potential, consider how your secret lapses of integrity (simply put, doing in private what you would never admit in public) have far-reaching effects on the consciousness and well-being of us all. In this verse, the ROADBLOCK of OLD IDEAS of denial, the fallacy that there are such things as victimless crimes, is exposed:

If the truth be known,
So connected we all are,
That we dare not harm a flower,
Lest we disturb a star.

One's twenty-first birthday is frequently the start of the reign of OLD IDEAS with all their attendant feelings of defeatism and confusion. By the time we have reached this gateway to adulthood, most of us have already begun to carry our autobiography in our head as a kind of internal hologram of who we are. Typically, this mental holographic image is comprised mostly of our fears, shortcomings and feelings of inadequacy, and serves as a kind of blueprint for a disappointing self-fulfilling prophecy. No matter how perfectionistic we might have been, most of us at twenty-one have not been Miss America, drafted by the NFL, discovered by a Hollywood talent scout, won an Olympic gold medal, the U.S. Open or Wimbledon. By twenty-one, most of us have a nagging feeling that we ought to be further along than we are, and we begin to secretly question whether we'll ever fill the shoes, or the chair, or the expectations of our role models and heroes. I had a client recently remark to me, "It's amazing how many of us adults are actually running around with internal self-images of ourselves as children!" I couldn't agree more. Despite the size of suit or shoes we may wear, probably most adults are actually living with the ROADBLOCK of OLD IDEAS of ourselves, feeling like imposters, terrified that eventually someone will catch on that we are not really competent, not really grown up. Driven by the sheer panic of being exposed as frauds, we pedal as fast as we can so that we won't be found out!

I remember when I was twenty-one, upon graduating Phi Beta Kappa from the University of Arkansas, I felt a palpable sense of, "Now what?" as I looked into the uncharted future with no roadmaps or milestones in sight. The structure that a formal education afforded me had fallen away into a shapeless sea of personal and professional options for which I felt completely ill equipped. While my own collection of OLD IDEAS of myself as a student was dominated by positive self-descriptions, it was woefully lacking in concepts of how I might relate to the rest of life. On the one hand, academia was a world in which I had tasted excellence and had some considerable modicum of personal reward. But on the other hand, the business world was completely foreign and seemingly hostile to me, a place I was not at all eager to approach, just yet. So, like lots of young people, I plunged headlong back into academia, the world that had been my home for so long, and completed a year-long course of study in Spanish culture at the University of Madrid and then a masters degree in Spanish Literature at New York University. In this case, my OLD IDEAS of self came in handy, temporarily, as they propelled me through two of the most fascinating and enriching pursuits of my life, graduate studies in Madrid, Spain and a masters degree from New York University in Literatures of Spanish authors.

OLD IDEAS for me were also filled with unmistakable overtones of "people pleasing" and I found myself continuing with doctoral studies upon return to the United States, partly because of school being a comfortable "parking place" and partly to please my parents, friends and husband. OLD IDEAS that the world was a hostile and competitive place and that I would never measure up, coupled with my self-image of the "hero" child from a military family was consistent with pursuing a doctorate, my self-fashioned equivalent to my father's rank as a Colonel. My personal OLD IDEAS were compounded by the centuries-old cultural OLD IDEAS I had been exposed to for three years in Spain in which women were truly second-class citizens, falling into the Madonna/whore dichotomy, and receiving respect from mostly only their adult sons and valued merely for their ability to procreate. For me, pursuing a doctorate was tantamount to the challenge of a lifetime, as I took on the OLD IDEAS of the Women's Movement during an era in which professions for women were an easy choice. One could become either a nurse or a teacher. Both professions were termed, "something to fall back on" in case "something happens" to one's husband. My personal feelings of inadequacy and vulnerability compelled me to "arm" myself with the title of "Doctor" and plenty of letters behind my name, in order that I might hold my own in the male-dominated world of business.

These personal illustrations of how OLD IDEAS help shape our lives point out that many times the outcome of operating on early self-concepts can be very positive indeed. The Fortune 500 is filled with CEO's who achieved their status, stock options and golden parachutes by following their autobiographical holograms all the way to the bank. Unfortunately, this same distinguished group is also filled with men and women who have become workaholics at the expense of their family lives and personal health. Many of our culture's megastars of television's "Pinnacle" and "Biography" reached their coveted destinations at enormous personal sacrifice and considerable tragedy. OLD IDEAS certainly have their usefulness, just like the clothing of yesteryear, but at some point in our lives, it becomes apparent that it is time for a change of mind. OLD IDEAS simply outlive their usefulness and need to be identified and laid aside.

As in the discovery of any ROADBLOCK, the shock of slamming one's life into an OLD IDEA usually leaves one no choice but to wake up to a harsh reality. For me, I had been hurtling headlong down the career path paved with OLD IDEAS of overachievement, overwork, and overlooking my own needs for five years as a licensed clinical psychologist before I hit the proverbial wall we call "burnout." For five years I sped along my career path guided only by the principle that "more is better" and by the delusion that I was somehow indispensable to my clients and had the obligation of seeing more per day, per week, per year than my health would allow.

I had become a consummate "professional codependent" and had lost my real identity along the way. To paraphrase an old recovery community joke, with each holiday or vacation opportunity not taken, the actual celebrations and adventures of my own clients would flash before my eyes! My OLD IDEAS had seduced me into a lifestyle that was no lifestyle at all. Taking no time for my real-life family, I had allowed my clients to become a kind of collective, surrogate family and their stories, dilemmas and dramas, a composite surrogate life that I was living vicariously.

Thankfully, assisted by a family medical emergency, I sought professional help for my codependency, the by-product of my own OLD IDEAS about my own identity and purpose in life. For me, the setting for this long overdue spiritual renewal was the peaceful snow-covered hills north of Montreal, Quebec. It was there, amidst the Laurentian Mountains, that I was able to restore my life to one worth living, as I examined every aspect of my past through the Twelve Step process. For me, it required the stunning blow of my husband's loss of his eyesight for me to begin to shatter the DENIAL about my lack of true personal direction and authenticity. Awareness came with plenty of pain, personal regret and humility. Looking at OLD IDEAS and exposing them to the light of day required for me, the assistance of wise and humble therapists who had themselves demonstrated the personal courage it requires to take stock of their lives and their own OLD IDEAS. Secure that I was among dedicated and loving professionals, each committed to a path of spiritual transformation, I found the strength to take inventory of my OLD IDEAS one by one, and surrender them to the recycle bin. This singular experience of surrendering my pride for the purpose of beginning the transformation process and restoring my joy is one for which I will always be grateful.

In the spiritual renewal center where I exposed and laid aside my OLD IDEAS, I realized how idiosyncratic and egocentric these tattered trappings can be. For most of us, it is our negative self-beliefs that we carry faithfully into our adult years, like a self-defeating "insecurity blanket." This phenomenon of selecting our flaws and secret failings, remembering our embarrassments, shame and guilt, and then weaving them into self-limitations, arises in large part, due to our missing the point that learning by trial and error is normal, that failing is as much a part of success as is victory. Psychologist Dr. Joyce Brothers writes, "The person interested in success has to learn to view failure as a healthy, inevitable part of the process of getting to the top," and Henry Ford deflated the false power of failure when he wrote, "Failure is only the opportunity to more intelligently begin again."

In my own codependency treatment program I discovered that one of the pivotal memories of my childhood and the source of many of my OLD IDEAS occurred on my eighth birthday, when, as an Air Force child, new to a very established and provincial neighborhood in Montgomery, Alabama, I had invited virtually my entire third grade class to my birthday party. Having spent only two months in this new school, I remember asking the teacher's permission to distribute hand-made party invitations in class, so that my new classmates would come to my party and become my friends. On the day of the big event, prepared for forty little guests, only one little girl arrived. Quickly, my parents called my two cousins from across town to come and save the day. Then both Mom and Dad jumped into action and gift-wrapped almost anything they could find and filled a laundry basket heaping full so that I would feel I was having a successful party. That night, as I was tucked into bed, I recall clutching tightly my new stuffed cocker spaniel from "Lady in the Tramp" and thinking before falling off to sleep, that, now that I was eight years old, maybe the carefree days of youth were behind me and life just might be pretty hard from now on. That day, November 21st, many years ago, was not only my eighth birthday, but the birthday of one of my personal OLD IDEAS—that I had to work extra-hard to fit in and to be accepted.

The particular OLD IDEA that life is full of rejection and that acceptance is unlikely, served to steer me away from further opportunities for rejection, such as trying out for cheerleader in high school as well as a number of other challenges. It wasn't until I started college that I began to go into overdrive in a surge of what clinicians call a "reaction formation" against this OLD IDEA that life was too hard and that success, achievements and popularity were for other people. Without consciously choosing the stellar college career that ensued, I found myself in a whirlwind of success, a virtual vortex of accomplishments and recognition—almost as a direct knee-jerk reaction to my intense fear of failure. By graduation I had been awarded "Outstanding Senior Woman," attained the highest Grade Point Average in the College of Arts and Sciences and named Miss Arkansas for the National College Queen Contest. The rewards of overcompensating for my personal fear of my OLD IDEAS were very powerful for me and served in their own right as the beginnings of a new OLD IDEA that perfectionism is good, healthy, and can lead to true success and happiness.

Another fallacious, yet ubiquitous OLD IDEA is that money makes people happy. Millions upon millions of individuals select careers based on this insidious ROADBLOCK, and tolerate pursuits they abhor to earn the almighty dollar, so they can be happy. In fact, the history books are filled with examples of truly successful individuals propelled into great achievements from their own fear of poverty, failure or shame. In each instance, those who transcended "workaholism" and achieved true personal success were able to examine their OLD IDEAS and make peace with a new, personally meaningful value system. While many legendary icons of success began their empires motivated by fear, the truly great individuals of history soon transformed their motivation into their love of their work. From Frank Lloyd Wright to Madame Curie, from Sam Walton to Bill Gates, the truly successful individuals among us have always been impassioned about their professions. Dale Carnegie wrote, "You never achieve real success unless you like what you are doing," and Kahlil Gibran wrote, "Work is love made visible."

The ROADBLOCK of OLD IDEAS, once examined, can be harnessed to allow you to live your life by choice, not by the chance of what might have befallen you as a young child. Many times, just by the sheer act of choosing to revisit OLD IDEAS and to select with discernment the valuable from the out of date, one can update one's dreams and open to living fully in the moment. This "right living" attitude of optimistic hopefulness and expectation of surprise opens up one's path to synchrony, that indefinable mystical phenomenon of meeting just the right person at just the right time, having a disarmingly unlikely confluence of events that open doors to worlds previously unimagined. Letting go of the ROADBLOCK of OLD IDEAS frees one up to living a life of limitless possibility, and once experienced, changes a person forever!

Recently, as I have begun employing clinical hypnosis with my clients, I have been reminded of the savage power of OLD IDEAS to derail our dreams and damage our self-esteem. Using age regression with one client, she and I discovered how an incident that occurred to her when she was a very young child shaped her sense of self so profoundly that she has felt powerless to change it for the past thirty years. This woman had, as a child, lost a sister in a fatal accident. Since that personal family tragedy, she had felt a very strong sense of responsibility to help her family shoulder the pain, survive the loss and carry on. Like most children, egocentric by nature, she had felt somehow responsible for her sister's death and took it upon herself to be the "provider" for her family. She took on the role of the "hero" and sought to rescue her several other siblings and her parents from adversity thereafter. This "savior" role that she lived out translated into her taking on the financial burdens of all her family members, going to great lengths to do everything for everyone else, and led to her consequent inability to allow others to do for her. In short, she too had hit the wall of burnout and was finally seeking professional help.

Clinical hypnosis was of great value to this exceptionally talented woman whose life story thus far reads like a "How To" book for success and fortune, but with the dark undertones of depression and sadness that stem from her feelings of hopelessness, knowing that she was living an "automatic life" rather than one of choice and feeling horribly trapped. Just as in the illustration of how my life had some of its own crescendos as the direct result of unexamined OLD IDEAS, this woman had made millions of dollars, created a sparkling career, impressive by anyone's standards, but at the ultimate expense of her own internal fulfillment and peace of mind.

Once she was able to relive through hypnosis the defining moment of her sister's death, she could finally see and appreciate the way OLD IDEAS of herself as rescuer had shut her off from a multitude of life choices that would have allowed her not only to give nurturance and support, but also to receive it from others.

Another exceptionally inspiring young woman came to me initially to address problems related to being unhappy in her marriage. As therapy progressed, and she began to explore the ROADBLOCK of OLD IDEAS that she had brought to the relationship, her therapy really began to take off. This young woman was highly accomplished, held an enviable and highly visible position at the university level, was extremely creative and a virtual pioneer in science and human relations in a large metropolitan city. Yet, somehow, she did not view herself as successful. Despite the fact that she had a naturally sweet spirit, an intrepid intellect and uncanny wit, she neither recognized her natural talents, her unmistakable physical beauty nor her sheer charismatic appeal. Somehow, she thought herself unattractive, even ugly. Her clinical symptoms included depression, anxiety and compulsive eating, as she had used food to medicate her feelings. Her therapy was marked by enormous courage on her part, as she unearthed harsh and searing memories from a tortured and lonely childhood. Up to this point, repressed recollections had haunted her, perversely disrupting her relationships with everyone she met, every goal she set, and, most importantly, distorting her own sense of self-worth.

For this remarkable woman, as so typically occurs, it was during a time of intense duress and personal crisis that ghosts of the past began to surface and make themselves known to her so that she could address the ROADBLOCKS of OLD IDEAS and set them straight, once and for all. For most of her life she had viewed herself through a kind of circus looking glass, with the ripples that distort reality, making even the most perfect image misshapen, twisted and distorted. During therapy, this young woman dared to begin to see herself as others see her. Ever so gradually, and with touching and poignant personal recollections, she began to expose the lies that she had lived with her entire life, the distortions of reality that had blinded her to her beauty and talent, limiting her to feelings of personal limitations and painful disappointment with herself.

At one point in her therapy I recommended that she might write a letter to her inner child from her own concept of a Higher Power, in order to address the fearful parts of herself that had persisted as a natural, if vestigial survival mechanism. Her letter is so eloquent and moving that I asked her permission to use it with her name changed. Her letter has touched thousands already as I shared it during several of my lectures, on audiotapes and television. Speaking from her viewpoint of her perfect parent, her concept of God or someone capable of loving her unconditionally, this is what she wrote:

Dear Sweet Rebecca,

It's safe to come out now little one. No one is going to hurt you. Mommy and Daddy are gone now, and they can't hurt you anymore. I know Daddy looks so mean and scary — like he hates you and wants to kill you. I know you hate that belt. It hurts a lot

31

and the noise is so loud, and it's so humiliating when he beats you. I know what torture it has been for you to wait for days for him to get home in order to get punished for something you did while he was away. When you come home from school or a friend's house and see Daddy's car in the driveway, I know how afraid you are to go inside. And, when Daddy gets violent and runs over stuff with the car and slams doors and breaks things, it's very scary. When he throws food at you and stuffs it down your throat I know you are afraid.

No one has been there to help you or protect you. No one has been there to tell you that you are okay, that you are just a little kid, and that little kids do goofy things and make mistakes – that's how they learn. It doesn't seem that way though when Mommy turns on you. I know it hurts – all you want is to be loved and accepted. I know you feel like you must be horrible and like you've done something terribly wrong, but it's not true, little one. What you need to understand is that all the anger and hate that Mommy and Daddy express doesn't have anything to do with who you are or what you've done. You are good. You are pure and wonderful.

It's not your fault when Mommy and Daddy yell at night, and Daddy says he doesn't want to come home because of you. It's hard to escape from all that fighting and screaming – you can hear every word they say. Those words hurt and it's hard to go back to sleep. When Daddy stays in his room all weekend and Mommy gets mad at you, you think you've done something wrong. It's very important

*now, honey, to understand that you are not the
cause of their unhappiness. You are not the reason
their marriage is a mess.*

*It feels like there is no one to love you. There has
been no one to read to you, no one to go shopping
with and look at dolls with, no one to help you with
school, no one to talk to, no one to take care of you
when you were sick or hurt.*

*You feel ashamed because you have no nice clothes.
You feel like you don't deserve anything nice
because Mommy complains that she never has
anything nice because she has to spend all the
money on you. It hurts when Mommy says you are
ungrateful, selfish, and that you always want too
much. It hurts when Mommy says you are ugly, fat
and a little slut.*

*You feel afraid to participate in school because
Mommy doesn't want to get involved. You feel like
you would be betraying her by being accepted. You
feel afraid to have friends over because you don't
know what Mommy and Daddy will do. Will they
get in a fight in front of your friends? Will they beat
you and your friends up?*

*You feel like you have been a very bad little girl and
the worst thing that you ever did was start that fire
in the field. You think you are now doomed for life.
Mommy said you had disgraced the entire family
in front of the whole neighborhood. Mommy said the
only reason Daddy didn't kill you was because
grandpa and grandma were there. Mommy says that
no one starts a fire in a field and gets away with it.*

It hurts when Mommy blames you for ruining her Christmas and her birthday. It was confusing to find all the pornography and then to get in trouble for looking at it. And, when you were afraid because poison ivy made your eyes swell up and you had to go to the hospital, Mommy said she was embarrassed to be seen with you. You really needed reassurance then.

So, you see, it is not strange that you believe you are ugly, fat, and that you have been a slut. You think you are selfish if you do not always give in to others and that you don't deserve to have anything nice. You believe you are damaged for life. You certainly don't need anyone to help you because you have become an expert of taking care of yourself.

You certainly can't talk about your feelings to anyone because that would probably ruin Mommy's day and Daddy would probably smash you for it. You feel like you ruined the family's reputation by starting that fire, and as a result, you will pay for that for the rest of your life. You feel like you are no good. Whenever anyone is upset or angry, you take responsibility for it and you run for cover. It feels like all men are capable of being violent and all women will eventually betray you. It feels like you are at the mercy of all these people.

But from here on out, things will be different, my sweet child. Because I want you to understand that Mommy and Daddy were very frightened when they did all those things – just like you have been. You see, they are very sick and can't tell what they are doing. You are just a child and children start fires because they are curious about matches. There was no one there to watch you and you were just being a regular kid. You couldn't have known what would happen. Mommy said all those things because she was afraid she and Daddy would get in trouble or that you could have been seriously burned. But she didn't know how to express those fears. Neither did Daddy. Whenever he was afraid, like you are now, he would lash out.

I'm taking care of you now, and together we will be the perfect picture of health. We will have whatever we want, and we will no longer be limited in our thinking about what we should have or do.
We will surround ourselves with other happy and healthy people, and we will create only the most peaceful and joyful experiences in our lives.

At this very moment, we come to believe that the world is a friendly place in which to live. Even though Mommy and Daddy and other people may be very sick, we will always take care of ourselves.

God is our real Mommy and Daddy, and we've just been confused. From now on we will let God take care of us. It will be fun! We will listen to Him and do what He wants us to do. I promise to take good care of you and treat you just like a sweet, little girl deserves to be treated. You deserve all those wonderful clothes, all those frilly and good smelling things. You deserve to be pampered and cared for always. From now on, we will be the best of friends and we will always know that we are whole, precious, and good and that we deserve only the very best that life has to offer.

Love always,

Rebecca

As Rebecca demonstrated so eloquently through her letter, written as though from her perfect Heavenly Parent, childhood incidents, internalized feelings of not just making a mistake, but being a mistake, and the shame that ensues can have a devastating effect on one's life. The fallout from exposure to childhood trauma can contaminate one's life and deform one's self-image for decades. The residue from a childhood of fear, pain and feeling unloved tends to cloud one's vision of the possible, and leave one with feelings of uncertainty and unworthiness. Rebecca's letter serves as a sort of collective prototype for the thousands of letters from their Higher Power that my clients have written over the years on their own respective journeys towards self-awareness, forgiveness, and the courage to start anew and with a fresh slate.

OLD IDEAS is an equal opportunity ROADBLOCK. It does not discriminate between the famous and the rest of us. For many of us, our ROADBLOCK of OLD IDEAS might not seem as monolithic and strikingly poignant as was Rebecca's. Our childhoods might have been rather wonderful, our parents, loving and devoted; and yet, to a person, each of us faces OLD IDEAS that we must expose and dispose of, in order to exercise freedom of choice about our life's journey. The mere fact that none of us is capable of seeing ourselves as others see us is a source of warped perception and OLD IDEAS. Even more compelling is the fact that none of us is fully capable of envisioning our full potential. None of us can completely map our destiny or know what may lie just around the next curve. Our lives, fluid as a river, are filled with surprises, obstacles and opportunities. Our OLD IDEAS are ever-forming and ever-changing, presenting us with the moment-to-moment challenge to view life with new eyes and update our images of our purpose and ourselves.

Frequently, the hallmark of OLD IDEAS is what is referred to as "external locus of control," signifying the unfortunate tendency to give away power to external circumstances and individuals, rather than to maintain and cultivate personal power. An example of this squandering of personal choice and power might be the OLD IDEA captured in the reasoning, "If I had a million dollars (or, these days, a few billion) I'd be happy," or the OLD IDEA, "Someday my prince will come (and I'll be happy)." Examples of OLD IDEAS might include such thoughts as, "More is better," "I'm not good enough," "I must please other people," "People will like me better if I'm perfect," "Some people are just born to succeed," and "Successful people never had difficulty." Most OLD IDEAS have to do with distortions of our self-perceptions and flawed reasoning related to how to perfect ourselves, or at the very least, begin to feel worthy. OLD IDEAS are earmarked by flawed reasoning and faulty logic. When OLD IDEAS govern our thinking, we distort the relationship between cause and effect. The Greek poet and philosopher Sappho captured the actual relationship between virtue and beauty when he wrote, "What is beautiful is good and who is good will soon be beautiful."

OLD IDEAS usually lead us to attempt to impress other people, and in our immaturity we still create idols and icons for ourselves, individuals whom we would like to dazzle. Then, just like children, we knock ourselves out to see our success or failure reflected in their eyes. Emerson writes,

"It is easy to live for others; everybody does. I call on you to live for yourselves."

Similarly, some of our most influential beliefs about spirituality and religion also fall into the category of OLD IDEAS. Throughout my years as a clinician, I have been struck by the preponderance of my clients who, when asked to comment on religion or spirituality, answer in a way that proves that they continue to operate from OLD IDEAS.

Most of us first thought of God or a Supreme Being when we were extremely young children, perhaps only two or three years old. So, with the mental capacity of a toddler we first pair the word "God" with a concept that a toddler can understand, a concept that is concrete in nature. Many of us at that tender age, began to visualize God as looking like our actual father. Perhaps we recited the Lord's Prayer that begins, "Our Father, Who art in Heaven," and automatically associated God with "Daddy." For many adults, especially those with dysfunctional childhoods, there is a hangover effect. This association of a Supreme Being with one's earthly father when unexamined, may result in the OLD IDEA that religion must be rejected along with the trappings of youth and especially the dependency of childhood. What is a natural dynamic of maturation and individuation, moving from infancy to adulthood, can actually carry with it, unintended beliefs and reactions, simply from failing to update our belief system. Like throwing the baby out with the bathwater, many of us speed through life with precious little time to contemplate, much less upgrade our values and beliefs. The results can be dramatic and sometimes dangerous, as our belief systems are the foundations upon which we build our lives.

The OLD IDEAS related to spirituality exist on another plane beyond the individual, as, typically, in our culture, God takes the form of an old guy with a white beard, someone that looks like Santa Claus, only in a white robe and living in the sky, sitting on a cloud. We were told that, like Santa, He was up there somewhere and He was watching us all the time. We learned that God (like Santa) "Knows what you've been thinking, He knows when you're awake, He knows if you've been bad or good, so be good for goodness sake!" In short, this God character took a lot of fun out of what we wanted to do when we were two or three, seven or eight—into adult life and beyond.

With OLD IDEAS being the way they are, unexamined belief systems, probably a majority of adults today still carry at least some of their emotional reaction to this overarching, anthropomorphic figure into their adult years and reject (or at least turn their Sunday morning backs on Him, accordingly, saying, invariably, "Oh, I believe in spirituality, just not organized religion." This powerful OLD IDEA generalizes for most of us to include other people we might consider to be authority figures. I am continually amazed by the reaction formation of most of my clients who complete the sentence stem, "Authority figures" with, "I don't have any!" Much of this rejection of religion or authority stems directly from the phenomenon of OLD IDEAS. In this case, our mental images on these subjects were programmed by a two or three year old and haven't been updated in any fundamental way since.

As we grow, develop, and mature into emotional literacy, we accept the challenge of taking responsibility for thinking for ourselves. We ask questions, challenge assumptions, update our knowledge and begin to create for ourselves a comprehension of reality that is marked by wisdom, grounded in fact and experience and one which supports our reaching for the stars and becoming fully human and in touch with the spirit that fills us.

By definition, OLD IDEAS are rarely characterized by wisdom, and often are evident when we are living a life of trivial pursuit—emphasizing achievements and their by-products fame and fortune, rather than the principles of living that create true happiness. Goethe wrote, "Things which matter most must never be at the mercy of things which matter least," underscoring how the material world often mesmerizes us while the ethereal world of spirit and principle may elude our conscious attention. Most of us recognize our OLD IDEA that reality is material rather than spiritual only after our failure to live a life based on values and principles has led us to crash and burn.

A common and very seductive OLD IDEA is the belief that there are actually instant, "just add water and stir" formulas for fulfillment, satisfaction and feelings of finally having arrived. Many a mid-life crisis is fueled by the misconceptions that by earning an academic degree, moving into the big new house with the proper ZIP code, having X number of dollars in one's bank account, or marrying Mr. (Ms.) Right, one will achieve the desired emotional and mental state. There may be no more apt a recent example of the fallacy of this OLD IDEA than the explosion and demise of the Dot-Coms that had immeasurable global impact, both financially and personally for millions. It is incredibly tempting to latch on to the "happiness formula du jour," if you will, the kind that are splashed all over the magazines at the check-out counter promising the impossible in just three easy steps. We tend to feel flattered when we are described as being "romantic" or possibly a "dreamer." It has become fashionable to be on a fast track to success, whether in matters of the heart or merely physical fitness and sex appeal. The

ROADBLOCK of OLD IDEAS stops us in our tracks when we place our faith in shallow and mechanical imitations of fantasy.

"Just what does happen when a fairy tale is being used as a script for one's real life?" you may be asking. I think this to myself when I see people throwing themselves into debt to stage a world-class wedding, only to pay for it with interest during the early years of their marriage. Over the top weddings always signal in my mind a kind of OLD IDEA hangover, which often results in other over-the-top behaviors from other OLD IDEAS.

Just for the sake of making the point unforgettable, consider this little ditty by an unknown author:

Rindercella Story

Once upon a time in the Kairy Fingdom lived Rindercella and her bad sisbetter and her three sugly isters. And the prandsome Hince in the Kairy Fastle threw a bancy fall because he was loving for a looker. He invited all the mair faidens in the Kairy Fingdom, all except Rindercella. Her bad sisbetter and her three sugly isters went on to the bancy fall to prance with the dancesome Hince and it didn't look like Rindercella was going to get to go. Ah! but all of a sudden in a light of boltening appeared her Mairy Fodgother and she said, 'Oh, Rindercella, you will go to the bancy fall and prance with the dandsome Hince and love into fell. But you gotta remember that when the midstrikes clock night you'd better beat it out of there before you turn into a pruneseed.' And with a wand of her

magic wave she transformed Rindercella into a
bing of feauty. She wore a gancy fown and a pair
of slass glippers and off she went and did she ever
prance with the dancesome Hince. All of a sudden
the midstrike clocked night and Rindercella was a
good girl and did what her Mairy Fodgother told
her, and as she was stepping down the go off came
one of her slass glippers, but she kept on running.
And with this the prancesome Hince came down
and picked up the slass glipper and he said, 'Oh,
my love, my life, the one whose foot fid dit this slass
glipper will be my Pairy Fincess and rule the Kairy
Fingdom forevermore!' And off he went through all
the Kairy Fingdom trying to find the mair faiden's
foot that fit dit the slass glipper. And he tried it on
everyone, even Rindercella's bad sisbetter and the
three sugly isters and it fid't dit. Why, they all wore
size twelve in a boot. Well he tried it on
Rindercella, and, of course if fid dit. And the storal
of the mory is, if you want to go to the bancy fall
and prance with the dancesome Hince and love into
fell and become the pairy frincess forever more,
when you're stepping down the go, don't forget to
slop your dripper!

Pretty silly, huh? But every fairy tale, even twisted ones, have morals. In this case, the "storal of the mory" is that each of our own OLD IDEAS is a ROADBLOCK to reality, opportunity and fulfillment. Do you have any fantasies (best-suited for bedtime stories) that you've been taking out a mortgage on, working two jobs to support or simply going crazy to make happen?

If you can think of even one of your personal OLD IDEAS, you can now update it and make it serve your real needs

better. Since our OLD IDEAS are usually our "wants" that
we mistakenly think are our "needs," part of the maturation
process is moving us from the wishes of children to the reality
of adults; sorting out our "wants" from our "needs" and
getting on with our lives and getting done with the nonsense.
This process is far from the killjoy exercise that it may sound
like. Au contraire. When we can distinguish our dreams
from the objectives necessary to reach those dreams, we are
able to take a short cut to our goals. We actually begin the
goal-achieving process in a realistic manner and avoid the
pitfalls of excess, addiction, distraction and ultimate
disappointment.

If we have any remnants of the OLD IDEA of a natural or
overnight success, we can upgrade our desires to realities
by adding the elements of discipline, sequencing, focus and
dedication. Knowing that a masterpiece and virtually all
priceless accomplishments are 10 percent inspiration and
90 percent perspiration is a great comfort. The OLD IDEA
held so tightly by children in make-believe and magic is
replaced by a belief in ourselves, our perseverance and the
value of our goals. Mark Twain put it this way, "The miracle,
or the power, that elevates the few is to be found in their
industry, application, and perseverance under the promptings
of a brave, determined spirit." OLD IDEAS might be viewed
as the raw material from which we carve out the building
blocks to construct our own personal monuments to our lives.
We must sort through them carefully, pick and choose the
best ones, and evaluate their relative value for our project.
Some are rough around the edges. Others are flawed by
fissures, and too weak to support a grand structure. No matter
how we look at our OLD IDEAS, we must accept our
responsibility to choose and shape the ones that will help us
create a thing of beauty of our life. I am particularly fond of
a verse by R. L. Sharp, which illustrates this:

REMOVING YOUR ROADBLOCKS

Isn't it strange
That princes and Kings
And clowns that caper
In sawdust rings
And common people
Like you and me
Are builders for eternity?

Each is given a bag of tools
A shapeless mass
A book of rules,
And each must make
Ere life is flown
A stumbling block
Or a stepping-stone.

"O" is for OLD IDEAS

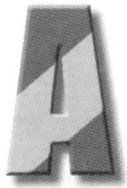 **is for APATHY**

"I want to feel myself part of things, of the great drift and swirl; not cut off, missing things; like being sent to bed early as a child."

Joanna Field

is for "APATHY." Webster defines "APATHY" as meaning "without feeling," "privation of passion, emotion or excitement; insensibility; indifference." When we are apathetic, it's as though wasted opportunities don't really matter. We're living under the delusion that today is merely a warm up for tomorrow when somehow, as if by magic, we will awaken to the reality of the fleeting nature of time and we will actually begin powering towards our goals and living with meaning, purpose and direction.

When we are apathetic, we are living as though the following statement is truth:

This life is a test; it is only a test.
Had it been an actual life
You would have been given instructions as to
Where to go and what to do!

Many of us live our lives as though they are merely dress rehearsals for the real thing. We use words like, "getting by," and "making do," "it's good enough for government work" and "Thank God it's Friday!" to sum up our collective ennui. It reminds me of some college courses that are well known for their degree of exactitude and difficulty, classes like statistics or physiology, classes that many students opt to take on a "pass/fail" basis, or avoid all together, so as not to risk lowering their grade point average. Perhaps even more apropos is the example of taking filler courses like underwater basket weaving, courses selected for their utter lack of content and challenge. Many of us think we will be happier if our life is easy, every day a "slam dunk" or a "gimme." We mistake our shying away from challenge with false feelings of safety and security, only to be hit head-on by our mid to late twenties with the emotional pain of the imposter syndrome or the fear that others will discover our cowardly streak and expose us. APATHY detours us from our inner dreams, and places us on a slow road to disappointment and boredom. One of the great women leaders of our time is Sarah Weddington, who spoke of the power of passion, meaning and contribution. In her words, "Life is not just making a living but having an impact beyond ourselves."

When we live our lives without passion, without putting it all on the line, we end up with something that feels like this:

There once was a pretty good student
who sat in a pretty good class,
and was taught by a pretty good teacher
who always let pretty good pass.

He wasn't terrific at reading,
He wasn't a whiz bang at math,
But for him education was leading
Down a pretty good path.

He didn't find school too exciting
But he wanted to do pretty well.
He did have some trouble with writing
And nobody had taught him to spell.

When doing arithmetic problems
Pretty good was regarded as fine,
5 + 5 needn't always add up to 10
A pretty good answer was 9.

The pretty good class he sat in
Was part of a pretty good school,
And the student was not an exception,
On the contrary, he was the rule.

The pretty good school he attended
Was there in a pretty good town,
And nobody there seemed to notice
He could not tell a verb from a noun.

The pretty good student was part of
A pretty good mob.
And the first time he knew what he lacked
Was when he looked for a pretty good job.

It was when he sought a position,
He discovered that life could be tough,
And he soon had a sneaking suspicion,
That pretty good might not be enough.

The pretty good town in our story
Was part of a pretty good state
Which had pretty good aspirations
And prayed for a pretty good fate.

There once was a pretty good nation,
Pretty proud of the greatness it had
Which learned much too late, if you want to be great,
Pretty good is in fact pretty bad!

I find that this ROADBLOCK of APATHY is particularly
pesky and pervasive, partly since it has received international
sanction in its many and diverse forms, not the least well
known of which is its embodiment in the "couch potato."
Whether in televised beer commercials or mass marketing

to sullen and sulking teens, the apathetic consumer is Everyman and Everywoman, a kind of cultural paragon of dour sophistication, too cool to care, too calloused to be concerned.

I have noticed in clinical sessions over the years that much of this apparent indifference to the truly Herculean challenges facing us in the world today is born of a sense of being overwhelmed by the enormity of the problems that we are exposed to on a moment to moment basis, through the airwaves of the media. Bombarding us at every turn are global, even universal problems requiring our attention and solution. Even the most caring among us is bound to feel daunted by the tasks at hand, helpless and insignificant. This feeling of "Why try?" results for many of us in a general feeling of malaise, a kind of collective "low grade depression" if you will, the symptoms of which are isolation, low energy, procrastination, avoidance, and a low sense of personal satisfaction with ourselves and our lives—in short, APATHY.

Horace Mann recognized this tendency among us to put off living our life, to fail to seize the day. He wrote:

> *Lost: One 24-hour, 24-carat golden day.*
> *Each hour studded with 60 diamond minutes*
> *Each minute studded with 60 ruby seconds.*
> *But don't bother to look for it.*
> *It is gone forever;*
> *That wonderful golden day*
> *I lost today.*

The ROADBLOCK of APATHY, let's remember, is a ROADBLOCK precisely because of the stuff APATHY is made of—an absence of passion! Two different people might seem to live the same day, go through the exact same motions, but experience two completely different realities. One might be marked by APATHY and the other by pure joy, total enthusiasm and a mindfulness of the precious nature of the day. The first individual would lose a 24-hour, 24-carat day, by utter unawareness of its priceless value, while the second would create and share the joy of the gift of the "present" with everyone she meets.

The person who lives fully, enthusiastically, consciously even the simplest of days, finds joy in every second, meaning in every minute. The individual who can marvel at the most mundane, find magic in the ordinary, is blessed beyond words, and has transcended the ROADBLOCK of APATHY. None other than Albert Einstein once wrote, "The fairest thing we can experience is the mysterious. It is the fundamental emotion that lies at the cradle of true art and true science. He who knows it not, who can no longer feel amazement, is as good as dead, a snuffed out candle."

One of my favorite verses by a poet named Donna Jane Tappert expresses this very well:

I Find Joy

I find such joy in simple things:
A word that rhymes, a bell that rings;
A pen that writes while upside down,
A laughing child, a loving clown;
A sweet old lady's sweet old smile,
Two friends who build a back fence stile,
Ah, friends! Such joy? A loving touch,
A smile, a hug, it won't take much
To make my cup of joy fill up,
And splash around. Come bring your cup,
If yours feels empty, bitter, blue—

REMOVING YOUR ROADBLOCKS

I'll share my joy—that's what I'll do?
Come help me count my blessings, friend
No need to die until "The End"
Not even then, for life goes on?
I know it does—God wouldn't "con"
His children of His lovely Earth—
He gave us laughter, joy, and mirth—
He wouldn't jerk it all away
'Cause we were "bad"—just made of clay
And prone to "sin"—or miss the mark.
This isn't just a place to park
While God adds up our bads and goods,
Subtracts our "might have beens" and "shoulds"
And if we haven't done too well says,
"That's too bad. Now, go to Hell."
Ridiculous! But I digress—
We're counting joys and happiness:
Like cats and dogs, and baby pigs,
And music, singing, dancing jigs!
And pies and cakes and stuff like that
(Those candy bars that make us fat)
And friends so kind that they will say,
"So what? We love you anyway!
We love you big. We love you small.
Or ugly, handsome, short or tall.
Don't worry if your nose is long.
Come join us in our grateful song."
We're singing of our many joys—
Come women, men, and girls and boys,
Let's understand that joy and fun
Should be in life for everyone.
And counting blessings helps a lot—
Like ice cream (cold) and coffee (hot)
And teachers, preachers, plumbers too,
And telephones, in beige or blue;

And paisley prints, and nice perfume,
And rainbows, birds and plants that bloom
And roses, squirrels, butterflies,
Hot air balloons in peaceful skies.
I find such joy in simple things:
When I enjoy my life has wings!

APATHY, therefore, is a highly complex ROADBLOCK, a kind of conglomeration of perfectionism, feelings of inadequacy and inferiority, self-doubt, lack of direction, fear of taking a risk, childlike beliefs that some "grown-up" out there is going to take us by the hand and help us get where we want to go. APATHY, then, is life without passion, tinged with regret.

In this discussion of APATHY, I am reminded of one of my favorite phrases. Many of us go through life "majoring in minors." In our avoidance of significance, we engage in the trivial pursuit of everyday activities, meaningless motions and repetitive tasks. We empty and fill the dishwasher, mow the yard, pay the bills, wash the car, do the laundry, punch a clock at work, collect a paycheck and haul the family to an annual "vacation" and call it a life. When these time-killing activities are carried out without passion, we are apathetic and we tend to feel inadequate, unimportant and quite small in the greater scheme of things. People caught in this daily doldrum existence tend to abide by Charles Schultz's famous maxim, "I'm learning to dread just one day at a time."

A friend of mine had a five-year old son who unwittingly coined a word for that sense of dread of the future marked by anxiety and pessimism. He called it "anticipointment." I think that many of us, shadowed by memories of past let downs, personal failures and painful recollections of times we enthusiastically plunged into life's deep end, only to belly flop, be laughed at or have loved and lost, know deep down precisely the nagging feeling of anticipointment. Anticipointment is a universal phenomenon, a stranger to none of us. Anticipointment may just be the five-year-old part of us that shrinks from significance, feeling inadequate to reach beyond our grasp. Anticipointment is that part of APATHY that watches as we pass by the brass ring on the carousel of life without so much as attempting to reach out and grasp it.

An anonymous author penned the fate of those who let anticipointment dictate their level of achievement:

> *Some men die by shrapnel,*
> *Some go down in flames.*
> *But most men perish inch by inch*
> *Playing little games.*

As a culture, we are collectively accustomed to referring to ourselves as being "terribly busy." If our television commercials accurately capture this high-speed, treadmill-existence we call life, we are harnessed, hobbled and hassled by the very technology designed to provide us convenience, leisure, quality time for our families and the pursuit of meaningful activities. Driven by our avoidance of our own potential greatness of achievement and creativity, most of us find ourselves on very short leashes to our pagers, cell phones, fax machines, laptop computers and stock market quotes, ever in a reactive mode and rarely if ever free to pursue our dreams, face our own dragons and reach deep inside ourselves for the proverbial stars. We leave the adventure of taking risks and making waves up to the actors on the silver screen and pacify ourselves with a vicarious identification with the likes of Kevin Costner in "Field of Dreams," Roberto Benigni in "Life is Beautiful" or Jimmy Stewart and his epiphany in "It's a Wonderful Life."

Mark Twain reveled in poking fun at a nation of procrastinators, as he admonished, "Never put off until tomorrow that which you can do the day after tomorrow." Peter Drucker recognized decades ago this tendency to avoid the plague of perfectionism and stated, "You should concentrate on doing the right things rather than doing things right." Alfred E. Newman was keenly aware of the emptiness that results from APATHY. He wrote, "Most people don't know what they want but they are pretty sure they haven't got it," and also, "If you don't know where you're going, it doesn't matter if your alarm doesn't go off!"

So a life marked by the ROADBLOCK of APATHY is stalled out, going nowhere in particular. There is an old Chinese proverb that captures this predicament:

Unless we change directions
We are likely to end up where we are headed.

Perhaps you have enjoyed the ironic silliness of the Parable for Procrastinators, which goes like this:

This is a story about four people named Everybody, Somebody, Anybody, and Nobody. There was an important job to be done and Everybody was sure that Somebody would do it. Anybody could have done it, but Nobody did it. Somebody got angry about that because it was Everybody's job. Everybody thought Anybody could do it, but Nobody realized that Everybody wouldn't do it. It ended up that Everybody blamed Somebody when Nobody did what Anybody could have done.

So it seems that the ROADBLOCK of APATHY is marked

by the delusion that as individuals, islands unto ourselves, that our thoughts and dreams, our courage or lack thereof somehow stand alone, not influencing a sea of others. In actuality, the phenomenon of "The Hundredth Monkey" postulated by the famous biologist and professor, Dr. Rupert Sheldrake describes the inescapable interactive nature of our "private" thoughts, acts and dreams. Dr. Sheldrake termed his adaptation of "The Hundredth Monkey" phenomenon, the "theory of the morphogenetic fields" (mass consciousness). In short, he posits, when a large enough portion of the population accepts something, it becomes a standard.

"The Hundredth Monkey" phenomenon was discovered by scientists who, for over thirty years had been devoted to studying the habits of a species of Japanese monkeys living off the coast of Japan. In 1952 the scientists began to provide these monkeys with sweet potatoes, dropped in the sand. Soon, these sweet potatoes became the monkeys' daily dietary staple. The monkeys liked the sweet potatoes, but found the dirt and sand unpleasant. One day, on Koshima Island, an 18-month-old female monkey named Imo went to the water's edge and washed off dirt from her sweet potato. Soon, she began to teach other monkeys to wash the dirt off the sweet potatoes before eating them. Between 1952 and 1958, this imitative behavior continued, as more and more monkeys on Koshima learned to wash their sweet potatoes before eating them.

The story becomes truly striking when, one day, once a critical number of monkeys (let's say 100), had begun this practice, suddenly all the monkeys in the tribe began to wash their sweet potatoes, without directly learning from others as imitators of Imo had. Furthermore, on the *exact same day* reports came in from scientists on outlying islands that colonies of monkeys on other islands as well as the mainland troop of monkeys at Takasakiyama started the practice of washing dirt off sweet potatoes, all without direct observation or any measurable means of communication!

Dr. Sheldrake's "theory of morphogenetic fields" is captured in his statement that there exists "an intelligent transcendent quality in the Universe that is holographic and omnipresent throughout nature." He believes that "memory is carried outside of one's brain," and admits that, on other levels, his theory is akin to Carl Jung's theory of the "collective unconscious" as well as to the concept of "cosmic evolution" proposed by paleontologist and Jesuit philosopher, Teilhard de Chardin.

In stark contrast to Sheldrake's theory, in our APATHY, we usually feel quite separated from one another, indeed, quite invisible and insignificant, as though our own evolution of conscious is somehow inconsequential. When we shrink from significance and the limelight, we reason that, at least, our fear of failure is not noticed and our acts of omission probably don't amount to much. We pacify ourselves with a feeling that someone other than ourselves will somehow accomplish the really important things in life, the cure for cancer, the remedies that will save the environment, the artwork or literary masterpiece that will lift the spirits of humankind and inspire us to greatness. In our APATHY we are living lives of loneliness and alienation, as though there were no collective unconscious, no morphogenetic fields through which we are all connected and constantly communicating. Little do we know that our cowardice, our APATHY just as our courage and initiative, are actually contagious. The great British metaphysical poet, John Donne, captured the essence of our connectedness when he wrote, "No man is an island entire of itself; every man is a piece of the Continent, a part of the main... And none other than psychologist William James opined, "No living person is sunk so low as not to be imitated by somebody."

APATHY, then, comes from the fatalistic feeling that one is insignificant, incapable of making a true mark on the world. It results in an attitude of, "Why try?" The following facts fly in the face of this defeatism:

> *By one vote Hitler won leadership of the German Nazi party in 1923.*
> *By one vote Congress saved the U.S. Army from instant collapse by voting on August 12,1941 to extend the Selective Service Act of 1940 (about to lapse) for another 18 months – less than 4 months before the Japanese bombed Pearl Harbor.*
> *By one vote Thomas Jefferson won the American Presidency over Aaron Burr when the election was thrown into the House of Representatives.*
> *By one vote Rutherford B. Hayes became President over Samuel Tilden in 1876.*
> *By one vote Texas was admitted to the Union in 1845.*
> *By one vote Andrew Johnson was saved from impeachment.*
> *By one vote the English language was chosen over German for America in 1775.*
> *By one vote a Texas Convention elected Lyndon B. Johnson over Ex-Governor Coke Steven in a contested senatorial election in 1948.*

It seems to me that those of us who lull ourselves to sleep on the couch of life with a six-pack and a bag of potato chips mistaking this out-picturing of APATHY as our simply being "normal" are settling for an unlived life. Willing to be "Joe Average," we let APATHY block our futures from view and we settle for network programming, unaware that we are having an impact, if only by omission of any creative activity, on countless others.

I have a theory, born of my own personal experience and that of clients of mine over the years, that APATHY results in part from the deeply held belief that we have already missed the bus! We fall prey to the tendency to confuse reality with what we see in the media. We note the youth of movie stars, rock stars and political leaders and feel that it must be too late for us to accomplish anything of significance. Unaware of the fact that multitudes of the world's great artists, authors and leaders made their greatest contributions later in life, we are resigned to that private disappointment of being left behind. For me, there may be no greater sense of personal tragedy than to feel deeply the desire to make a positive difference in the world, to help people you will never meet, to see the world, write the books and plays, the songs and even letters—only sadly, to feel that you have missed your opportunity.

I've always been encouraged by stories about late bloomers and if there were ever an antidote for APATHY it is a good book full of stories about these remarkable people. Among the most obvious late bloomers is the artist Grandma Moses, a farmer and homemaker from Upstate New York whose first offering was noticed in a drugstore window when she was 78, and her first big breakthrough came two years later when she was 80 with a one-woman show. By the time of her death at the age of 101, she had created over 1600 works of art, and her legacy remains one of the most sought-after among American art to this day. In the realms of literature, the favorite American author, Laura Ingalls Wilder, beloved creator of the *Little House on the Prairie* and the seven other "Little House" books, did not begin her career as a novelist until she was in her mid-60's. The message we glean from the achievements of ordinary people doing extraordinary things is that it is never too late. In the words of Grandma Moses, "Life is what we make it, always has been, always will be."

Here it is important to distinguish activity marked by passion, awareness and purpose from activity marked by reactivity, passivity and emptiness. APATHY, let's remember is characterized by indifference, a lack of passion. One can be outwardly very active, seemingly successful and busy, while actually moving through space and time without taking pleasure and finding purpose in life. Another might appear peaceful and content, and possibly involved in a low-prestige lifestyle, and still live each day with full appreciation of life, a sense of value-added, aware that one has made a difference.

The distinction between APATHY and enthusiasm appears to be one of consciousness, not a comparison of personality "type B" with "type A." Just as often as not the apathetic one is the person in high gear, the "type A" personality who might be climbing the corporate ladder or keeping up with the Joneses. The high-speed, sensation-saturated life of the "type A" Superwoman or Superman might be secretly serving to medicate feelings of inadequacy and to avoid true intimacy. These apathetic individuals in disguise know how to numb their feelings through excessive activity and feelings of outer self-importance. All the while, they are unwittingly keeping a lid on their true identities as spiritual beings by their dedication to being "human doings" rather than "human beings."

APATHY is a state of mind, in fact, more precisely, a lack of mindfulness. It is indifference to the inevitable purpose of our existence. The masks it wears are legion. What gives it away is the secret feeling of giving in to a personal cowardice from facing ourselves and our true nature. APATHY is abdicating our accountability to develop ourselves as fully as we can while we walk this planet, to transform ourselves and our lives.

Raymond B. Fosdick realized the value of overcoming the daily seduction of APATHY as he wrote of "The Adventurous Life":

> *The only life worth living is the adventurous life.*
> *Of such a life the dominant characteristic is that it*
> *is unafraid. It is unafraid of what other people*
> *think. Like Columbus, it dares not only to assert a*
> *belief but also to live it in the face of contrary*
> *opinion. It does not adapt either its pace or its*
> *objectives to the pace and objectives of its*
> *neighbors. It thinks its own thoughts, it reads its*
> *own books, it develops its own hobbies, and it is*
> *governed by its own conscience. The herd may*
> *graze where it pleases or stampede where it*
> *pleases, but s/he who lives the adventurous life will*
> *remain unafraid when he finds himself alone.*

We can't help but continue to be inspired by the immortal words of Napoleon Hill in his classic book *Think and Grow Rich*, "Whatever the mind of man can conceive and believe, it can achieve."

It seems obvious that Robert Frost was also keenly aware of the impact of his own convictions on all humanity as he wrote,

> *My goal in life is to unite my avocation with my vocation*
> *As my two eyes make one in sight.*
> *For only where love and need are one*

And work is play for mortal stakes
Is the deed ever really done
For heaven's and for future's sake?

I noticed the power of enthusiasm and value-added life while on a cruise to the Orient. One afternoon in a restaurant in Tokyo, we were served lunch by a lovely young Japanese woman. We were discussing the remarkable and charming qualities of the people we had met on the streets of Tokyo, when our waitress came to take our order. As if in keeping with our marveling at the courtesies of so many Japanese people who had helped us, served us or simply greeted us during out sightseeing that morning, this young woman epitomized a custom in Japan referred to as "Kata."

At the head of our group and our table that afternoon was the late, great teacher and inspirational speaker, Jack Boland. Jack was leading a conversation at the table in his inimitable style, by marveling at the many admirable qualities of the Japanese people, which had impressed us during our stay. Jack had a way of expanding the tiniest of everyday miracles or wonders and helping others notice and appreciate them. Just as he was beginning to write down these qualities on a paper napkin, the young Japanese woman attending our table appeared gently, with a sweet smile and offered him a notepad and a pen to facilitate his writing. She bowed slightly as she approached, and again upon departing. Her gestures were graceful and fluid, transforming the mere provision of writing materials into an act of kindness, thoughtfulness and generosity of spirit. This is "Kata."

Throughout the meal we noticed her manners, her demeanor and her dedication to serve us our meal. What had occurred was so much more than delivering a meal to a table. We had witnessed and been changed forever by "Kata," the value-added tradition that translates into our culture as, "It's not so much what you do, as how you do it."

APATHY, then, is the absence of "Kata." Enthusiasm is its opposite—the awareness of the potential gift within each moment, each gesture, each thought. The antidote to APATHY, then, is enthusiasm—awakening to one's purpose and to one's opportunities to make a contribution. It is assuming a higher consciousness and the ability to marvel at the infinite and the eternal all about us. It is the enlightened soul and its mortal offspring, passion.

I wonder if the young woman we met in Tokyo will ever have any idea of the impact her enthusiasm and joy of serving others has had on me and those in my party. It is not likely that she even gave her actions a second thought, as, indeed, it was not her actions, but her consciousness that made all the difference. It was her quiet and gentle passion that communicated and transformed the day, indeed the entire trip, for all of us.

Each of us is entrusted with the responsibility of making our mark, making a difference, and shaping the universe with our own transformation of consciousness. Few of us realize the reality of this invisible, spiritual power and most are distracted, even mesmerized by the grosser, material world and how it appears to work. It is easy to succumb to the numbing effects of the material world and fall prey to the ROADBLOCK of the APATHY that results from such a limited perspective.

A short anecdote from Broadway illustrates the difference between an awakened and consciously passionate individual from one who is asleep to his responsibilities in life. One evening backstage, a fatigued Mary Martin was in her dressing room preparing for her starring role in South Pacific. She had performed in this legendary role to rave reviews for thousands of performances, and was feeling somewhat uninspired that evening, when a messenger arrived backstage to deliver to her a hand-written note from the composer Oscar Hammerstein, who was in the audience. The note was short, and it read:

A bell is not a bell until you ring it
A song is not a song until you sing it;
And love was not put in your heart to stay
For love is not love until you give it away.

This simple note touched Mary Martin's heart like no other, and the energy and passion with which she performed that evening astonished the audience. Of course, her inspired performance was followed by a standing ovation, and the power of Mr. Hammerstein's encouragement and passion continues to ripple through the ages. Even as you read this page, you are changed by his message of inspiration.

APATHY is not so much the absence of action, but of true passion and the vitality of feeling fully alive. This ROADBLOCK is one of omission. APATHY is evident when one is not cognizant of one's blessings, not conscious of the daily miracles that occur unnoticed throughout our every waking moment. APATHY is evident when we are self-absorbed, and when we fail to marvel at the intricacies of human kindness, gestures of generosity, moments of courage that fill the sea of humanity all around us. When we are facing the ROADBLOCK of APATHY, it's as though we are asleep. When we replace APATHY with enthusiasm, we put our life and daily bothersome details into perspective and are grateful for even the problems that we face.

I remember feeling the full impact of this fully conscious perspective one morning in Warren, Michigan, as I sat in an audience of thousands and listened to the legendary author of *The Greatest Salesman in the World*, Og Mandino, as he read one of his favorite poems that help us awaken to the joy and gratitude that make life worth living. It is entitled, "Lord, Forgive Me When I Whine" and goes like this:

Today, upon a bus I saw a lovely girl with golden hair, I envied her . . . she seemed so gay . . .and wished I were as fair. When suddenly she rose to leave, I saw her hobble down the aisle. She had one leg, and wore a crutch. But as she passed . . . a smile! Oh, God forgive me when I whine, I have two legs. The world is mine.

I stopped to buy some candy. The lad who sold it had such charm, I talked with him. He seemed so glad. If I were late it would do no harm. And as I left he said to me, "I thank you. You have been so kind. It's nice to talk with folks like you. You see, he said, "I'm blind." Oh God forgive me when I whine, I have two eyes. The world is mine.

Later, while walking down the street, I saw a child with eyes of blue. He stood and watched the others play. He did not know what to do. I stopped a moment, then I said, "Why don't you join the others, dear?" He looked ahead without a word, and then I knew he could not hear. Oh, God forgive me when I whine. I have two ears. The world is mine.

With feet to take me where I'd go, with eyes to see the sunset's glow, with ears to hear what I would

know . . . Oh, God forgive me when I whine. I'm
blessed indeed. The world is mine.

Clearly, we remove the ROADBLOCK of APATHY by filling ourselves with enthusiasm and living with passion. No act is insignificant, no task, boring and no human being unrelated to ourselves. This feeling of "He ain't heavy, he's my brother" begins to lighten our load and we become aware that each of us is made of "star stuff." With our eyes wide open, we embrace the present and appreciate every minute:

Just a tiny little minute
Only sixty seconds in it
Forced upon me. Can't refuse it.
Didn't seek it, didn't choose it,
I must suffer if I lose it,
Give account if I abuse it.
Just a tiny little minute,
But eternity is in it.

"A" is for APATHY

 **is for DENIAL**

*"I'd like to make a motion that
we face reality!"*

Bob Newhart

is for DENIAL. The fourth ROADBLOCK is the detour of DENIAL, a barricade that brings all forward progress to a screeching halt. When DENIAL is one of our personal ROADBLOCKS, it is our own disbelief in the existence of a shortcoming or failing within ourselves. DENIAL may be likened to a scotoma, a blind spot in our field of vision. Just as the organ of vision, the eye has scotomata or blind spots on the retina, each of us suffers perceptually from various blind spots about our personalities, our impact on others, and the parts we play in the interpersonal conflicts of our lives. DENIAL is, then, a kind of collective blind spot regarding our responsibilities and accountabilities in life, the ways in which we trip ourselves up, self-sabotage, and create realities for ourselves that we don't like and then tend to pin the blame on someone or something else. DENIAL is fueled by false pride, the need to be right, and by egotism, an exaggerated love of self.

DENIAL brings out the truly ridiculous in all of us. We see it all around us as though we were all members of the flat earth society, treating other people like commodities, acting as though we were immortal. Sometimes, as I am writing my progress notes in my office following a session, and reflect on the endless varieties and forms that our DENIAL can take, I would find it amusing, were the human stakes not so high.

DENIAL is the fraternal twin of BLAME and, in fact, is akin to each of the ROADBLOCKS. DENIAL is a kind of pervasive defensiveness that is so omnipresent that quite often we don't even recognize it. Just like fish in a fishbowl on a search to find water, most of us are surrounded by our own personal DENIAL, unable to see it. Being defended against the ugly truth of our shortcomings is such a familiar condition for us that we do not even recognize it as the ROADBLOCK that it is.

As a clinician, I often see DENIAL most vividly in relationship counseling, as each member of a couple feels misunderstood, mistreated and helpless, as though he or she were not a co-creator of the relationship's distress. In couple's counseling, DENIAL appears first in the finger-pointing version of "He said, She said." During this dead-end of an exercise in futility that author and therapist Robert Subby brilliantly termed "trivial dispute," neither party can accept responsibility for their own shortcomings. The walls of DENIAL must come tumbling down before any real progress is made.

DENIAL relies heavily on false pride to maintain itself in the face of mountains of evidence that one is in fact, not without faults, flaws or frailties. DENIAL is usually the strongest when the individual has the poorest self image, the lowest self-esteem and the most fragile of identities.

DENIAL tends to give way gracefully to acceptance when an individual begins to "disidentify" from one's behaviors and commits to seeing himself as others see him. When the quest for the truth supplants the defense of one's false self-image as flawless and without blame, DENIAL loses its value and is replaced with valuable new information about oneself and the opportunity to make changes in order to develop and evolve.

In the recovery community of Alcoholics Anonymous, Codependents Anonymous and other Twelve Step programs,

Mark Twain's quip, "Denial ain't just a river in Egypt!" has become practically a cliché." Of course, DENIAL of one's addictions is the very centerpiece for the interventions and the target of all treatment center therapies. In fact, the mere identification of the dynamic of DENIAL, and the realization of the fact that it is universal among us and a kind of natural defense mechanism, are usually the true beginnings of a new and authentic life, one filled with humility and willingness to make amends for the daily shortcomings we discover within ourselves.

In removing the ROADBLOCK of DENIAL we must face our childish belief in the possibility of perfection among mortals, and replace that naïve viewpoint with the awareness that each of us is a spiritual being going through a human experience. By definition, then, as humans, we are walking the planet during this lifetime to work towards perfecting ourselves through often-painful events. As such, we must accept the spirituality of our imperfection and learn to value the fact that we are adequate, worthy, valuable human beings, even though we are all flawed, frequently floundering, yet all the while in the process of discovering our true nature and purpose. An old country song sung by Billy Joe Shaver seems to sum this up in a very simple image, with the words, "Oh, I'm just an ole chunk of coal, but I'm gonna be a diamond someday!"

As we begin to recognize the ROADBLOCK of DENIAL, we are already well on our way to removing it, for it is one of perception. If we do not see it, it will stop us in our tracks. Once we recognize it for what it is, we are free to take stock of ourselves in a daily inventory of character flaws and character gains, and begin to appreciate our progress, rather than acting out the delusion that any of us is already perfect or shall be during this lifetime.

Oddly enough, most of us developed a kind of perfectionism as a direct result of childhood lessons which were taught to us innocently enough through school guidelines, parental expectations, the archetypes of fairy tales, and via our television sets broadcasting images of fresh-faced boys and girls living in picture perfect worlds of Ozzie and Harriet or Beaver Cleaver and his family. Whether you remember "My Three Sons," "The Donna Reed Show," "Father Knows Best," or "The Brady Bunch," television was the national window into these scripted examples of surrealistic perfection that most of us accepted as desirable and, naïvely, even possible.

None of the television families I recall from the '50's and '60's featured adults recognizing serious personality flaws, taking stock of the harm they had done, making amends to others and then going to work to reinvent a new way to live. In short, DENIAL sold shampoo, automobiles, breakfast cereal and just about everything else we were consuming in those days. We saw "the USA in (our) Chevrolet" and bought hook, line and sinker the on-screen romance of Rock Hudson and Doris Day. DENIAL is as American as apple pie. During World War II we watched the matinee idols of John Wayne and other white-hatted cowboys fight the "bad guys," the ones in black. We are a culture of black and white, good and bad, a dualism in which there are absolutes and, in those days on the silver screen, the good guy always won. Only during the past few years has it been popular to explore the depths of the individual and to expose the conflicting elements within each of us. No longer nearly as naïve a collective society as we once were, DENIAL seems to be giving way somewhat to reality, and we are seeing more exposes of the way real people really are, in such shows as "Behind the Music" and other studies of the complexities that make us who we are.

When I was a very young child my mother used this little rhyme to remind me that I was both as fine and as flawed as my playmates:

> *There's so much good in the worst of us*
> *And so much bad in the best of us,*
> *That it hardly behooves any of us*
> *To criticize the rest of us!*

There is possibly nothing so irresistible as the naked truth, the exact opposite of DENIAL. I recall vividly the powerful magnetism of groups of women discovering their own truths about their lives, relationships and feelings during the 1970's while I was a student in Madrid, Spain. It was then that I first became fascinated with the field of psychology, as groups of women met informally in each other's homes to explore their own realities, dispel myths, discard OLD IDEAS, and shatter their respective DENIALS.

It was the explosion of the Women's Movement internationally that sparked my interest in forming thirteen "Consciousness Raising" groups in downtown Madrid— groups designed to allow women to meet together and discuss freely and openly their lives, feelings and commitments to change. That was the first time in my entire life I had ever heard frank discussion among adults of the way things really were for them, with them, and how they really felt about themselves, their marriages, their careers, and their futures. The contrast between what I was hearing and what I had seen in the media was so startling, that I made a commitment to formalize my training as a group facilitator by entering a doctoral program in psychology upon returning to the United States.

It was then as I began to discover my own ROADBLOCK of

DENIAL, and as women all around me were simultaneously discovering theirs that my career took a sharp right turn from my graduate degrees in literature to the applied science of psychotherapy in a private practice of psychology. I felt very strongly then that I had reached a fork in the road. Off to one direction, the one for which I was the most formally prepared academically, the road led to the study of the written word, the prose and poetry of both English and Spanish speaking cultures. I had long been enamored of literature, offered a full fellowship to complete my doctorate in English studies, and after living in Spain for three and a half years, ready to embrace a doctorate in comparative literature. Such was my love affair with the Spanish culture. Yet, even so, once I witnessed people around me, being real with one another, dropping their shields of defensiveness, their pretense of perfectionism, I knew that somehow I had to take the other road, the one I knew the least, the one that beckoned to show me who I really was and who I could eventually become.

I began to discover that it is true—truth really is stranger than fiction, and far more compelling. I began to explore with others the personal failings that I had kept secret and was shocked to realize that with disclosure of my failings and insecurities, I was embraced, warts and all. By being open and honest, I felt much closer to the women in the groups, in deed, to everyone I met. I began to have more realistic impressions and expectations of others, as my own self-perception became more clear and more honest.

The ROADBLOCK of DENIAL for me simply had to be faced in my early twenties, even though breaking through it required shattering reality as I had constructed it. I had held tightly to both idealism and perfectionism throughout my college years in the provincial hills of Fayetteville, Arkansas in the late 1960's. There we lived in a kind of time warp, shielded even from the harsh realities of the Viet Nam War and the national protests, from race riots and urban unrest. There, amidst the glorious autumn leaves of the Boston Mountains in northwest Arkansas, I plunged myself headlong into my studies and positions of leadership among service organizations of the University and embraced the pursuit of excellence.

During college, even though I was in DENIAL about many layers of reality, I was driven to succeed by the stark terror of failing. I recall clearly one early September night, a meeting in the university dorm when my freshman class was informed that by Christmas, at least thirty percent of us would have washed out and been sent home. Unaware that I was being driven by the myth of perfectionism, I applied myself as I had never done before, to my studies, my civic responsibilities and to my social relationships. Free from any illusion that I was particularly gifted or intelligent, I merely pedaled as fast as I could and began to see with palpable relief that I was not going to be among the group sent packing at Christmas. It was as though I had absolutely no relational global positioning system regarding my potential or my abilities, and I overcompensated in every area, in order not to fail. Instead of washing out, I made a straight "A" average that year. Motivated by feelings of inferiority and insignificance, I began to achieve, reach goals and raise the bar for myself again and again.

It was an unforgettable moment in time for me when I learned first hand, that "where there's a will there's a way." Compelled by my own personal fear of failure and a high sense of duty, (after all, I saw college as my "job"), I catapulted myself through four years of single-minded dedication toward achieving every goal in my path. With each successful attempt to make a name for myself, I was increasingly surprised, even shocked, that I was attaining such goals, goals that, at that time, I assumed were beyond my reach.

Part of my DENIAL system was the belief and inner perception that I was so insignificant and so ineffectual in the "world of grown-ups" that others would never actually recognize my efforts. My DENIAL included elements of my belief system in which I felt immature, even invisible, and most certainly not really real or significant. Apparently this sense of being so insignificant that one is actually invisible is, in no way, idiosyncratic to me. I have heard countless variations on the theme from my clients over the years. Feelings of having missed out, not measuring up, having life pass one by, and being all alone are fairly universal derivations of Alfred Adler's concept of the inferiority complex. They are also at the very foundation of Existential Psychotherapy, and the very core of the classical writings of the world's great philosophers. Somehow knowing that we are not alone in feeling alone is oddly comforting, and also helpful in removing the ROADBLOCK of DENIAL.

There is a story that captures this feeling and illustrates the DENIAL that distorted my perception of the world for years on end. It goes like this:

One day at a small town diner, a family of three was seated at a booth looking over a lunch menu. The waitress approached the table and began to take the meal order, starting with the mother, then the father, who ordered first for himself and then for his little four-year old son. The father said, "He'll have the child's plate with steamed vegetables and milk." The waitress listened, waited, paused, and then politely addressed the little boy directly. "And what would you like for lunch, young man?" she said sweetly. The startled four-

76

year-old boy looked up with a smiling face full of freckles and said, "I want a hamburger, french fries and a chocolate milk shake!" After the waitress left, the little boy turned to his parents and, with a broad smile and a look of utter surprise, blurted out, "She thinks I'm real!"

My personal taste of excellence during my college years was my awakening to that very feeling, "They think I'm real!" This odyssey through an identity crisis resulted in my being honored as Outstanding Senior Woman, Who's Who in Colleges and Universities, graduating with the highest grade point average in the College of Arts and Sciences and representing my state in the National College Queen Contest for leadership, scholarship and service. They say that one's strengths are also usually one's weaknesses. In short, even when one is in DENIAL, living with a blind spot to one's inner needs and feelings and even to the bigger picture for society in general, meaningful personal victories are possible. This brief collegiate history of mine merely illustrates that we are capable of circles of DENIAL within DENIAL. The Socratic injunction, "Know thyself" applied during the years I was an undergraduate at the university. At that time, the truth I sought was on a smaller scale. I focused on excellence within my scope of vision at the university, and achieved it. At that time for me, DENIAL had to do with my peripheral vision, the blind spots I had regarding other realities beyond myself and my most immediate circle of influence at school.

Looking back, I realize that I certainly fell short of making the history books, the *Guinness Book of World Records* or even the evening news. In fact, in retrospect, my accomplishments were actually quite meager on even the smallest scale of things. They are significant in this discussion of DENIAL, however, for their sheer power to shatter my expectations, perspectives and self-limiting beliefs about myself—to shatter my DENIAL. It was not so much the recognitions or honors that made any difference to me, as the impact of being catapulted out of a small mindset into believing that anything is possible. A simple ten-day trip to the National College Competition lifted a college senior out of the Ozarks in Arkansas to the Waldorf Astoria in New York City, the halls of Congress, the White House, Cape Canaveral, and finally West Palm Beach for the nationally televised broadcast of an already long-forgotten contest. That single American Airlines round trip opened my eyes during the dawning of my adult life and helped me break through a layer of DENIAL. I started the trip still shrouded in DENIAL about my true nature, still feeling invisible, unimportant, somewhat unaccountable, and returned with a sense that my life choices mattered and that I could and must make a positive difference in my life. "From those to whom much is given, much is required."

Only when I left the cocoon of the University and moved to Spain did I see my own culture quite differently through European eyes as I read about Nixon, Viet Nam and "The Ugly American" in the "International Herald Tribune." Needless to say, this venture into seeing us as others see us helped me to grow up and remove the ROADBLOCK of DENIAL about the natural tendency among us all to be egocentric, ethnocentric and chauvinistic, rather than to take responsibility for failings and shortcomings collectively and make every effort to change, to improve and to make amends. The egocentrism so appropriate for children can outstay its welcome into adulthood and become egotism, even racism or sexism, unless we commit to a program of emotional literacy. Until we accept the fact that "higher education" is not limited to formal education, but continues throughout our entire lives, we are likely to limit ourselves to petty goals. Unless we take the opportunity to mature our personal pursuits of fame and fortune, we will inevitably lose the perspective of the "big picture." In our immaturity of consciousness, and DENIAL of our proper relationship to others, we will actually forfeit our responsibilities and opportunities to be of service and to make contributions for the greater good, what Alfred Adler discussed as the sign of a highly developed individual "social interest."

As I discuss DENIAL, I realize that the concept is so complex, involves such a layering of considerations that I am having difficulty wrapping my mind around it. A good time for analogy and metaphor. The most commonly used illustration of DENIAL in psychotherapy circles in that of "the elephant in the living room." While this figurative elephant sits unrecognized in the living rooms of our lives we might be dusting our furniture, writing our books, dressing our children or remodeling our kitchens. The elephant represents an unacknowledged problem or point of pain in our lives, something causing trouble, and requiring our attention, but being selectively ignored, as we busy ourselves with less consequential matters. Despite our DENIAL, the elephant eventually demands our attention as it threatens to topple our foundation. The elephant might be alcoholism, depression in a family member, or even some social issue such as the Viet Nam War controversy in the '60's, poverty in our own cities, or issues of neglect and abuse of the elderly—issues which hover above and about us. When we are in DENIAL, we are simply blind to the to the threat the elephant poses to our continued existence and our ultimate goals.

In my case, DENIAL as a young adult took the forms of an elephant both within my personal circle of influence and beyond. I was blind not only to social issues raging throughout our nation at the time, but also to my own struggle with an eating disorder. Rather than recognizing the danger signs of my need to resemble (then) Twiggy (and perhaps, now, Kate Moss or Ally McBeal) by starving myself, I confused my skipping meals and compulsive exercising with the stoicism I was studying from the classics. While I was embarking on a lifestyle that eschewed alcohol, drugs and premarital sex, I was also "purifying" myself right into a bona fide disease, an obsession with body image that would eventually threaten my health. Needless to say, I knew there was something wrong, but DENIAL required me to be secretive about my self-doubts and to pretend that being thin as a rail was just a natural result of my busy and ascetic lifestyle. I rejected the offers of family members for medical attention as being unnecessary, and I delayed attending to the underlying emotional issues that always drive any disorder until years later, when "the elephant" demanded attention and presented itself in the form of career burnout, stress and marital problems.

For most of us, we refuse to acknowledge the elephant until we have absolutely no choice whatever in the matter anymore. I was no different. Only when we have "hit the wall" or, in recovery terms, "hit a bottom," do we face ourselves as we really are, with the good, the bad and the ugly, and finally ask for help. Fortunately, this moment of facing our failures is, in fact, a turning point. John F. Kennedy wrote, "When written in Chinese, the word 'crisis' is composed of two characters—one represents danger and the other represents opportunity."

Ironically, once we acknowledge the obvious, that we are not yet perfect, but are spiritual beings going through a human experience and working towards perfecting ourselves, then and only then do we begin to demonstrate the human qualities of honesty, humility, purity of intent, flexibility, openness, and faith that constitute a really good person. All the while we were clinging to our DENIAL and living as though we couldn't be improved upon, we were mere shells of the people we were destined to become. And all the while, the only people we were fooling were ourselves. One of the biggest surprises when we break through the DENIAL of our character flaws and recognize them is the fact that everyone around us has known the truth, at some level or other, the whole time! We are always the last to know.

DENIAL encompasses the myriad of times we allow ourselves to have blind spots in our lives. A common example of DENIAL as a blind spot relates to driving an automobile. Most accidents occur when the driver "didn't see it coming," due to a blind spot built into the car itself. Or perhaps this blind spot came from the dry cleaning hung behind the driver's seat, blocking her view. The blind spot might have been created carelessly by the driver herself who may have been dialing a cell phone, putting on make-up or tuning the radio, only to run into a mailbox or an on-coming car. Each of these is an example of a form of everyday DENIAL that, while seemingly inconsequential and innocent, can prove fatal.

I find in my clinical work with my own clients that DENIAL for them is usually equally innocent. Their blind spots to their overuse of alcohol or casual, "social" use of other drugs, their neglect of health problems such as obesity or diabetes or even their refusal to acknowledge the hazards of unprotected sex and the risk of STD's and HIV all constitute areas of DENIAL that could prove devastating, if not life threatening.

Possibly more common examples of DENIAL have to do with the priorities these clients set for themselves and their families, or, better said, the way they arrive at priorities by default. In my private practice I treat a very high-functioning clientele, by professional standards, mostly individuals electing professional assistance in order to attain their goals more efficiently. Most of my clients are seeing me by choice for personal or professional development and are seeking peak performance work, executive coaching, sports psychology services or the latest in applied neuroscience. To a person, they are seeking to gain in greater self-awareness by choice. Most are well-educated and successful by external standards and are interested in improving aspects of their lives, which have become troublesome or dysfunctional in some way.

My clients have often distinguished themselves in athletics, politics, and business or in social circles and quite frequently encounter the ROADBLOCK of DENIAL as a lifestyle hazard. In their quest for excellence, they tend to "key hole" certain activities, projects, goals or achievements and dedicate a disproportionate amount of energy and attention to these, sometimes at the expense of their health, their families, their values, and their relationships. "Key holing," a variant of DENIAL, is quite common among individuals with the highest of standards and the best of intentions. In these cases, DENIAL is a ROADBLOCK of omission, as an elite athlete, an acclaimed business leader, a financial wizard or a social superstar actually fails by succeeding. Through "key holing" one's "To Do" list, one's goals or achievements, one very easily loses sight of the fundamentals of a happy life, the realities of one's inner spiritual or emotional needs, and through the ensuing DENIAL, risks losing the intangibles that form the foundation of a life worth living.

One particularly memorable example of "key holing" occurred on a perfect spring day when I discovered a newborn fawn in our front yard. I quickly realized that this infant fawn was covered with fire ants, as it lay instinctively still awaiting its mother's return. My husband and I rescued the fawn, cleaned off the swarming fire ants, and then took the frightened baby deer to the home of a wildlife rescue volunteer who had two bedrooms in her home devoted to injured wildlife. Relieved to know that this tiny fawn would survive after a shot and medication, I noticed that the volunteer's young daughter was waiting in the hallway, hoping that her mother would take her to Walgreen's to buy supplies for school. The volunteer joked that she was usually too busy with stray animals to make the errand run with her young daughter, and that usually, her own child would just have to forego the trip and do without.

I remember the stark scene of triaged wild animals, each caged in animal carriers or children's playpens, in various states of recovery in the suburban home of this kind, volunteer wildlife rescue worker. Just outside the door, in the darkened hallway, stood a small little girl waiting quietly, hoping to get her mother's attention, but almost resigned to being ignored once again. I commented to my husband on the irony of the neglect of this child by her mother, a good woman, clearly passionate about being a helper and a caretaker. Our afternoon with a baby fawn led to uncovering a clear-cut example of DENIAL, of how "key holing" even worthy accomplishments can lead to painful consequences, and later to lost opportunities and eventual regret for the family of the wildlife rescue volunteer.

Over the past decade, our culture has come to terms with dynamics such as the "dysfunctional family," "recovery" and "codependency" mostly from mass popularization through talk shows, public television and network television sit-coms. What we have created for ourselves, in a classically 21st

Century style of mass production and market-driven design is a sort of "Psychology-Lite." Our awareness as a culture of our addictions, and self-defeating behaviors such as codependency might be likened to processed food, more junk food than fine cuisine. Even in facing our demons of DENIAL, we have sandwiched the increasingly rare commentaries by the likes of Bill Moyers or Garrison Keillor between talking bullfrogs in beer ads and Victoria Secret supermodels wearing wings and lingerie, asking if we "believe in magic."

DENIAL is the ROADBLOCK that may be chiefly responsible for allowing psychology to be, not only the "study of the soul," but also psychology, the applied science, in fact, the mental health industry. With the most succinct definition of insanity being, "when we keep doing the same thing over and over again and expecting different results," DENIAL is maintaining the refusal to learn from our mistakes. Portia Nelson brilliantly captures one of the all-time best illustrations of DENIAL and its demise:

Autobiography in Five Chapters

I.   *I walk down the street.*
     There is a deep hole in the sidewalk,
     I fall in.
     I am lost . . . I am helpless.
     It isn't my fault.
     It takes forever to find a way out.

II. *I walk down the same street.*
There is a deep hole in the sidewalk.
I pretend I don't see it.
I fall in again,
I can't believe I am in the same place,
But it isn't my fault.
It still takes a long time to get out.

III. *I walk down the same street.*
There is a deep hole in the sidewalk.
I see it is there.
I still fall in . . . it's a habit.
My eyes are open.
I know where I am.
It is my fault.
I get out immediately.

IV. *I walk down the same street.*

V. *I walk down another street.*

 **is for BLAME**

*"People are not 'victims' of
their emotions or passions.
They create emotions to assist
them in the attainment of their
goals."*

Raymond A. Corsini

is for BLAME. The "B" in ROADBLOCKS brings us to "BLAME" which goes right along with the Cartesian reasoning that supports its twin ROADBLOCK of DENIAL. The dualistic reasoning process that creates such absolute characters as "the good guy" and "the bad guy" comes in mighty handy when we justify or rationalize blaming others when the worlds we have created for ourselves aren't working to our liking, when the realities we have ordered up for ourselves backfire. Why it just must be someone else's fault! Yes, BLAME is closely related to DENIAL, alright, a co-conspirator in saving face and avoiding responsibility for our own failures and our own shortcomings.

One of my all-time favorite parodies on the Twelve Steps pokes fun at the ROADBLOCK of BLAME:

The Twelve Steps of Insanity

1. We admitted we were powerless over nothing. We could manage our lives perfectly and we could manage those of anyone else who would allow it.

2. Came to believe there was no power greater than ourselves, and the rest of the world was insane.

3. Made a decision to have our loved ones and friends turn their wills and their lives over to our care.

4. Made a searching and fearless moral inventory of everyone we knew.

5. Admitted to the whole world at large the exact nature of their wrongs.

6. Were entirely ready to make others straighten up and do right.

7. Demanded others to either "shape up or ship out."

8. Made a list of anyone who had ever harmed us and we became willing to go to any lengths to get even with them all.

9. Got direct revenge on such people whenever possible, except when to do so would cost us our own lives, or, at the very least, a jail sentence.

10. Continued to take the inventory of others, and when they were wrong, promptly and repeatedly told them about it.

11. Sought though nagging to improve our relations with others, as we couldn't understand them at all, asking only that they knuckle under and do things our way.

12. Having had a complete physical, emotional and spiritual breakdown as the result of these steps, we tried to blame it on others and to get sympathy and pity in all our affairs.

During the therapy hour, I see the ROADBLOCK of BLAME paired with its twin DENIAL quite often in relationship counseling. It is a most foolish therapist that would allow a couple to waste their therapy time and money playing "trivial dispute." This silly and often agonizing prelude to the productive portion of the counseling process can be sidestepped if the counseling starts out on the right foot in the first place. In truly successful relationship counseling, the therapist asks each individual to begin the process of exploring his or her own strengths and weaknesses through a process of diagnostic discovery. Only after the client has begun the self-discovery process to expose any flaws or character defects she may be bringing to the relationship, and her partner joins in the process for himself, does the therapist structure the sessions to meet together to make amends for their respective part of the trouble and pain. If BLAME cannot be removed on both sides of the couch, sadly, the couple may be blocked from forward progress and mutual understanding.

As is the case of most of our ROADBLOCKS, BLAME stems from the emotional reasoning we develop in childhood, and, therefore, is sometimes extremely difficult to identify as self-sabotaging and, finally, to set aside. We have all heard children caught up in the blame game of "He hit me first!" "Did not!" "Did too!". . .When we experience painful situations with feelings of rejection, hurt, anger or sadness, we reason emotionally that we have been at the receiving end of an injustice. We may feel victimized by another's behavior, neglect, tone of voice or any of a number of other "wrongs," and may automatically assume an attitude of righteous indignation, feeling entitled to BLAME the person who "made us a victim." We see a cause and effect relationship and we want to BLAME the cause, which we connect, rightly or not, with another person. We shout within ourselves, "You made me . . .(fill in the blank—cry, feel hurt, angry, etc.)!" Hence, BLAME is a form of emotional artillery we carry about and feel entitled to employ out of sheer self-defense. It is common knowledge in treatment centers that individuals who play the "victim" role, are guaranteed to feel entitled to victimize others. In fact, sometimes we feel that if we do not BLAME the other person we will be playing the fool, acting like a doormat and failing to demonstrate adequate self-esteem. Much of the self-help literature from the '70's and '80's has unwittingly perpetuated the ROADBLOCK of BLAME by encouraging a generation of individuals to "BE ASSERTIVE!"

BLAME has been elevated to an art form through many social movements this century and last in which certain groups take turns assigning BLAME to other groups for their plight, in centuries past and present. BLAME always takes a "victim," and, if you read any newspaper or watch any television at all you know that being a "victim" has become a ticket to sympathy, attention, and, last, but not least, litigation! BLAME as a ROADBLOCK takes finger pointing straight to court, much to the delight of the trial lawyers. Our courts are a virtual logjam of BLAME. Our justice system is impotent to resolve what can be resolved only within the individual. The "victim" is the 21st century's protagonist, with the leaders, the entrepreneurs and the innovators taking a backseat. Our television docu-dramas and tabloid journalism programs feature the "victim" in prime time and make a case for the possibility that BLAME is an appropriate and adequate response to misfortune. Meanwhile, as "the squeaky wheels get the grease," the champions of the fight against cancer, the people overcoming all odds in the form of physical or mental disabilities to pursue their genius and to overcome adversity, take a backseat. Only recently in television series such as A & E's "Biography" have we seen persons showcased who have rejected BLAME as a waste of time and have thrown themselves completely into making a contribution for the greater good.

Successful people learn quickly the energy drain and toxicity of holding a grudge, of blaming others or shirking personal responsibility. Emotionally mature individuals invariably understand the innate fallibility of human nature and, knowing that they themselves are far from flawless, learn to have compassion for persons who might offend them or do them harm. One of my favorite examples of this sort of compassion was uttered in the movie "Hook" by the character Wendy, as she witnessed an unseemly outburst of rage on the part of Captain Hook, played by Dustin Hoffman. Rather than rushing to the ROADBLOCK of BLAME, she elected to feel compassion, as she lamented, "He needs a Mommy very, very badly!"

Emotionally mature people move especially swiftly to compassion and forgiveness. They commit to making something good out of something "bad." Sometimes they start with the multi-layered task of forgiveness, the way "A Forgiving Soul in Florida" did when writing to "Dear Abby." His comical recipe for demolishing the ROADBLOCK of BLAME goes like this:

> *The friend who ran off with your wife,*
> *Forgive him for his lust;*
> *The chum who sold you phony stocks,*
> *Forgive his breach of trust;*
> *The pal who schemed behind your back,*
> *Forgive his evil work;*
> *And when you're done—forgive yourself*
> *For being such a jerk.*

Once we "get it" that daily irritations are opportunities for innovation, improvement and discovery, we learn to expect the unexpected and face it with a smile. We learn to lean into our lives as though we were skiers, always leaning downhill, into the slope, and taking the moguls with flexibility and strength. We see our daily lives as opportunities to create beauty and to experience joy. I am especially fond of this verse entitled, "The Oyster," that really expresses an appealing alternative to BLAME:

> *There once was an oyster whose story I tell,*
> *Who found that sand had got under his shell;*
> *Just one little grain, but it gave him much pain,*
> *For oysters have feelings although they're so plain.*
> *Now, did he berate the working of Fate*
> *Which had led him to such a deplorable state?*
> *Did he curse out the Government, call for an election?*
> *No. As he lay on the shelf, he said to himself,*
> *'If I cannot remove it, I'll try to improve it.'*
>
> *So the years rolled by as the years always do,*
> *And he came to his ultimate destiny—stew.*
> *And this small grain of sand, which had bothered him so,*
> *Was a beautiful pearl, all richly aglow.*
> *Now this tale has a moral – for isn't it grand*
> *What an oyster can do with a morsel of sand?*
> *What couldn't we do if we'd only begin*
> *With all of the things that get under our skin?*

Christian D. Larson expresses this attitude of winners beautifully as he writes that it is his goal,

> *To forget the mistakes of the past and press on to the*
> *Greater achievements of the future.*
> *To wear a cheerful countenance at all times and give*

Every living creature you meet a smile.
To give so much time to the improvement of yourself
That you have no time to criticize others.
To be too large for worry, too noble for anger, too
strong for fear,
And too happy to permit the presence of trouble.

All of the world's great religions address the ROADBLOCK of BLAME and admonish those who point the finger before first assessing their own shortcomings. In the Bible, it is in the Scripture, Luke 6:41, that asks, "And why do you look at the speck in your brother's eye but do not perceive the plank in your own eye?"

After more than two decades as a clinical psychologist in private practice working with literally thousands of people who came to me to improve their lives, I am impressed by the absolute power of humility to roll away ROADBLOCKS such as that of BLAME. I have witnessed wonderful individuals as they struggle with the phantom of perfectionism, finding it impossible to move forward to true happiness as long as they felt compelled to be right and to BLAME someone or something else for their misfortune.

Many times, the ROADBLOCK of BLAME appears when an individual blames not others, but himself, unable to forgive himself for his mistakes. As a clinician, I have often felt enormously frustrated watching this struggle continue until, mercifully, the client realized that they could be good, if not perfect, could move forward and not fault themselves for not being there already. If we recognize that holding grudges against ourselves is a form of BLAME, and therefore a ROADBLOCK full of regret, resentment and the same emotional toxins that contaminate other relationships, we can see that it not only our right to forgive ourselves, it is our obligation.

Usually during the therapy process there is some spiritual awareness that allows one to take one's proper place in the universe and to be developed and matured, rather than being somehow magically perfect from birth. Usually there is some metaphor or analogy that comes to the rescue and speaks to the very soul of the seeker. It is often something simple and hackneyed, such as the image of a toddler first learning to stand, then to walk. This endearing image usually conjures up memories of a younger sibling or a son or daughter who was lovingly supported and encouraged as he or she stumbled and fell, tried again and again, until eventually, amidst shrieks of support and love, took her first steps. This youngster was never diminished in the eyes of loving relatives for "failing" to walk "correctly" on the first try. The thought of such a harsh reaction is patently ludicrous. It is often a simple story such as this that will speak to the heart and the emotions of the individual who has heretofore held unrealistically high expectations of herself, judged herself, and not been able to accept less than perfection.

So, oddly enough, our discussion of this fifth ROADBLOCK, BLAME is actually intricately intertwined with our ability to accept with humility the fact that we are constantly striving, ever falling short, never ceasing, as we evolve and develop ourselves spiritually. Yes, we are spiritual beings having a human experience.

BLAME is no longer necessary as a self-defense mechanism if we prefer to take responsibility and abide by Harry Truman's phrase, "The Buck Stops Here." Only by assuming responsibility for our part in any conflict, mishap or wrongdoing have we any power to be part of the solution. This twist on our instinctive tendency to pin the BLAME outside ourselves actually has the paradoxical effect to empower us to do great things and become great people.

As I meet new clients seeking professional assistance for a broad and diverse array of personal problems, I have been amazed that the single most sought after therapy goal is simply, "peace of mind." For over twenty years I have heard men and women, adolescents and even children express in their own words that if they could have anything they would have, "peace of mind." Regardless of whether they seek clinical hypnotherapy to assist with smoking cessation or weight loss, look for guidance after a breakup of a relationship, are in need of healing during a time of grief or loss or trauma, ultimately, peace of mind is what the vast majority are seeking.

Many times, the ROADBLOCK of BLAME, either of another person or of oneself, blocks one from attaining peace of mind, the goal so elusive, so near, and yet so far. Once they can identify what is within their immediate circle of influence and begin to heal within that circle, once they put on the personal blinders, just as a race horse uses blinders to focus on the finish line, only then do they begin to make the paradigm shift from feeling stuck and hopeless, alone and helpless, to feelings of encouragement and excitement about the journey ahead.

This verse by an anonymous author puts to rhyme the removal of the ROADBLOCK of BLAME:

> *If you were busy being kind,*
> *Before you knew it, you would find*
> *You'd soon forget to think it was true*
> *That someone was unkind to you.*
> *If you were busy being glad*
> *And cheering people who are sad,*
> *Although your heart might ache a bit,*
> *You'd soon forget to notice it.*

If you were busy being good,
And doing just the best you could,
You'd not have time to blame some man
Who's doing just the best he can.

If you were busy being right
You'd find yourself too busy quite
To criticize your neighbor long
Because he's busy being wrong.

There is enormous power in attending to one's own garden, blooming exactly where one is planted and letting be what is beyond one's immediate influence.

Another verse, this time by Edgar A. Guest, entitled "Sermons We See" discusses people who have recognized BLAME as the ROADBLOCK that it is, and have moved beyond it. These are the people who not only talk the talk, but also walk the walk. While the "victim" who makes BLAME a profession is usually quite verbose, Edgar A. Guest prefers the lessons of the person who has moved well past BLAME into high gear:

I'd rather see a sermon, than hear one any day,
I'd rather one should walk with me than merely show the way.
The eye's a better pupil and more willing than the ear;
Fine counsel is confusing, but example's always clear;
And the best of all the preachers are the men who live their creeds,
For to see the good in action is what everybody needs.
I can watch your hands in action, but your tongue too fast may run.
And the lectures you deliver may be very wise and true;
But I'd rather get my lesson by observing what you do.
For I may misunderstand you and the high advice you give,
But there's no misunderstanding how you act and how you live.

When we are faced with the ROADBLOCK of BLAME we are stopped in our tracks. When we BLAME another for our emotional reactions we are actually giving away our own personal power. When we BLAME, we assume the passive posture of "victim" and allow someone or something else to determine our mood, if not our actions. We are, therefore, short-changing ourselves, underestimating our abilities and assuming a powerless position, one of emotional immaturity, more appropriate for a small child than for a mature adult.

Eleanor Roosevelt reminded us, "No one can make you feel inferior without your consent," and Terry Cole Whittaker agrees and titled her book, "What You Think of Me is None of My Business." Even Dr. Wayne Dyer makes it a point to turn away from BLAME by recommending that we allow life to unfold without taking it personally and without judging. He recommends that we can each take responsibility for ourselves and our own karma, and further states that how people treat you is their karma and how you choose to react to how they treat you is your karma.

Yes, removing the ROADBLOCK of BLAME is essential if we are going to move on towards our goals and enjoy the trip. In the Twelve Step program, in treatment centers and in therapy, it is essential that a client identify the resentments or the BLAME that she has carried around for years on end. This identification process is called "taking an inventory" and constitutes the Fourth Step. Once the client recognizes the enormous toll that carrying these resentments has taken, she then identifies the character defects associated with her reactions to them and how they have stood in her way. Through this process of taking inventory of "the exact nature of our wrongs" we gain power over our circumstances. It is at this point that we eradicate BLAME as a ROADBLOCK and move beyond to forgiveness. While BLAME had chained us to the circumstances and people we had given our power to, forgiveness sets us free. Forgiveness is a gift we give ourselves, as it loosens the grip of resentment and allows us to create new pictures for ourselves and the storyline that we have called our life. With our new pictures, freed from the toxins of BLAME, we create new feelings, new internal self-images and we develop new and more functional patterns of thinking and behaving. By moving past BLAME and insisting on forgiveness, we free ourselves from any "victim" role and assume leadership in our own lives. Aristotle once wrote, "The beauty of the soul shines out when a man bears with composure one heavy mischance after another, not because he does not feel them, but because he is a man of high and heroic temper."

I like the words of Margaret McKeever Elliott that are entitled, "Be Careful." In reading them you can just imagine that she might have been faced with some obstacle, some affront or offense, was tempted to BLAME, but paused before responding:

> *I'm careful of the words I say*
> *To keep them soft and sweet*
> *I never know from day to day*
> *Which ones I'll have to eat.*

In cases where there really is an unacceptable behavior going on in a relationship, say, verbal or physical abuse, for instance, I am not recommending that one simply ignore it. BLAME is a poor substitute for taking responsibility for one's own behavior that either allows the abuse to happen in the first place or continue to occur. Usually, in any on-going relationship, the two persons involved are equivalent emotionally to one another. They stay in the relationship because of the mutuality of their issues and their learned patterns of emotional response. If there is an abusive relationship, one person has unwittingly or unconsciously selected the other as partner in order to work through unresolved issues of abuse from childhood.

Most people reject this theory outright at first, and then blanch as they realize the hidden truth within for themselves. We protest, "But I would never in a million years want to marry my father (mother)!" Somehow, if we are completely honest with ourselves, most of us actually do, and, if we abide by the theory that we are on the planet to learn lessons, selecting partners with whom to "get it right" has a kind of evolutionary logic to it.

Instead of BLAME, one might identify one's own "victim" behaviors and dare to change them. "Victim" behaviors are almost always the color of fear. Sometimes these behaviors may be as simple as avoiding conflict, fearing to stand up for oneself and failing to set healthy boundaries or "draw the line." BLAME is often merely a poor substitute for taking appropriate action, and stems from one's lack of courage to face the unknown. When one has the courage to act bravely, one acts from love rather than fear, and all things are possible. Mark Twain reminds us "Courage is resistance to fear, mastery of fear—not the lack of fear." Instead of BLAME, therefore, courage. Courage removes this ROADBLOCK clear out of the road.

There is an adaptation of the Serenity Prayer that seems to apply here, for people who stay with abusive partners are usually codependents guilty of "wishing and hoping they'll change." They are paralyzed by this waiting game and are played the fool by the abuser who knows that the seesaw routine of verbal/physical abuse followed by the honeymoon period is as addictive to the "victim" as a slot machine in

Las Vegas to an addicted gambler. The intermittent reinforcement of on-again, off-again kindness and cruelty is the most addictive kind of reinforcement. The "victim" is literally chained by operant conditioning to stay and "wish and hope" a little bit longer, soothing herself with negative alliances, friends she can complain to, even songs romanticizing this nonsense and elevating it to something noble and even sexy. "Stand by Your Man" has been the theme song of many an abused woman, who played the BLAME game sometimes and justified her cowardice with this twangy justification that helped her feel more romantic about the whole thing.

So then, the Serenity Prayer applied for the recovering codependent, no longer into BLAME goes like this:

> *God, grant me the Serenity to accept the people*
> *I cannot change,*
> *Courage to change the person I can,*
> *And the wisdom to know that person is me.*

"B" is for BLAME

 **is for LIMITATIONS**

"Do not fear confrontation.
Even when the planets collide,
out of the chaos comes the
birth of a star."

Charlie Chaplin

L is for LIMITIONS. "L" stands for the ROADBLOCK OF LIMITATIONS. I am referring, of course, not to actual real-life limitations, but to LIMITATIONS that are self-imposed, irrational notions that we carry within us about our perceived "dead ends," beliefs that stop us short of our dream destinations. One of the most compelling thoughts I have ever heard about how we create our own LIMITATIONS, I heard from a speaker who proclaimed boldly that each of us is doing and experiencing exactly what we are choosing for ourselves at all times. At the moment of impact of this radical claim, I found it outrageous and easily arguable and false. Then I began to think more carefully about its meaning. When we encounter the ROADBLOCK of LIMITATIONS, we are actually facing unchallenged boundaries within our own minds. Yes, there may be people who might agree with us about these LIMITATIONS, but that doesn't mean they are hard and fast or true in any absolute sense, merely that the people agreeing with us are probably stuck behind their own ROADBLOCKS of LIMITATIONS and misery loves company, even in a traffic jam on the road to personal fulfillment.

We crash headlong into the ROADBLOCK of LIMITATIONS when we live our lives reflected in the faces and eyes of people around us, when we define ourselves by things and people external to ourselves. It is in this act of "externalizing" that we sell out for acceptance and approval and eventually, compromise our values, lose our souls and become spiritually bankrupt. For many, the catastrophe created by crashing into this ROADBLOCK sends them careening toward intensive care in the form of a therapeutic intervention, either with a therapist they trust or on a get-away to a spiritual and emotional renewal center, where, if they are lucky, they awaken to a whole new way of living—for one's self, rather than for others.

Usually we can identify our own personal list of LIMITATIONS. As a girl I was encouraged to "Always let the boys win at games; they really like that." Or, "Let the boys show you how to do things; it makes them feel important." We learn to make other people happy, or we learn that it is possible to do this, by seeking approval, avoiding conflict and playing it safe. Once we get started on the discovery process of identifying our LIMITATION ROADBLOCKS, we recognize a multitude of them. They are couched in phrases that we call "self-talk" such as, "I'm too old to do that," or "I can't do that because I don't have the training," or I don't have the financial support to do that," or "That's too rich for my blood." Sound familiar? We learned through conditioning to put these LIMITATIONS in place when we heard people say things like, "Who do you think you are, anyway?" We certainly wanted to fit in, to be liked, accepted, approved of, so we ran with the pack, joined the club that accepts LIMITATIONS as a kind of membership requirement.

My husband just shared with me an example of LIMITATIONS that stems to his childhood years in South Texas. He told me that it's a well-known fact that ranchers on the giant cattle ranches often keep their cattle corralled using a single strand of electrified wire strung between two fence posts. After the cattle's first exposure to the electrified wire, they will usually stay within the confines of the fenced area, even if a single strand of twine replaces the wire, or sometimes when it is removed entirely. Cattle, like people, remember adverse experiences for a long time, and learn this LIMITATION as a way to avoid pain. LIMITATION, therefore, is the result of the conditioning process and is governed by the pleasure-pain principle. The fences that we build for ourselves are also usually invisible. They were put in place years before we recognize that we are holding back from our dreams, corralling ourselves within our comfort zones, no matter how uncomfortable they may be.

One of my favorite illustrations of the ROADBLOCK of LIMITATIONS relates to my cat. In our household, our "children" are the four-legged, feline kind, Sasha and Christie. Sasha, we have learned, is actually a Double Fur Norwegian Forest cat. She has rich, brown, tabby markings, a beautiful face, and so much fur that she resembles a giant bedroom slipper. Alas, it seems, Sasha also has a bit of an eating disorder. Sasha lives to eat. When Sasha had lived with us for about three years we began to put the cats into the laundry room at night to help keep them contained so they didn't keep us awake. One morning I opened up the laundry room door as usual and called the cats. Christie came running to eat her breakfast, but, remarkably, Sasha didn't race through the door to be the first at the cat food dish. This caught me off guard, because Sasha, as the "Alpha cat" had always been the first one to the food. She absolutely never missed an opportunity to eat. When I went to look for her in the laundry room, I found her all nestled down into a furry ball, as though sleeping—but she was nestled right in the middle of the kitty litter box! Needless to say, I was not pleased.

Now, here we had a situation where our prized pet was a mess and smelled horrible, so we took her to be groomed. We brought her home all fluffed and puffed, proudly sporting a little red and white checkered kerchief around her neck.

The next morning, I found her hunkered down again in the middle of the litter box! Realizing this was not a good pattern, and the fact that we seemed now to have an emotionally disturbed cat with an eating disorder, and now some sort of litter box fixation, I felt the strangest form of professional inadequacy. As a psychologist, I was thinking that I should understand this and be able to fix it in short order. But I simply could not figure it out! First, we tried separating the cats for a while, hoping Sasha would find a more suitable place to bed down. But each morning as I opened the door to the laundry room, I was greeted by the same sight, and smell, a ball of fluff in the litter box. I was beginning to think that Sasha must be quite insane, as cats go, although I'm not aware of any feline mental health diagnostic codes, because her preferred place to nap had become the litter box. She had a new and smelly habit, and seemed utterly satisfied with herself.

Finally, I gave up and took my hygienically and emotionally challenged cat to the vet. When I finally spoke with Dr. Tom, I told him, "Tom, this is really embarrassing. We have a serious problem with Sasha's behavior. She's sleeping every night in her litter box, and you can see for yourself, this just won't work. What is going on? Could this be due to some form of kitty rivalry? Could she be depressed or acting out some form of anger at us?" Dr. Tom just grinned and paused for the longest time. Finally, he said, "Jan, the reason Sasha is sleeping in the kitty litter box is because she wants to."

Now, I paid Dr. Tom for this wee bit of wisdom, and it probably serves me right for the times I've been theoretically correct but of absolutely no immediate assistance in providing answers for some of my own clients. There's actually a name for what had just happened between me and my cat's veterinarian who provided me frustration instead of answers.

They call it the Zeigarnik effect. That day I left with an unresolved problem in a state of frustration, motivated to discover a solution. Theoretically, the Zeigarnik effect is actually the tendency for the frustrated client to discover the solution on her own, if adequately upset and motivated.

It turns out that what Dr. Tom was telling me is that Sasha had established a weird kind of comfort zone, a place that was familiar to her, stinky though it was. For all of its negatives, at that point in time, the kitty litter box was serving as a familiar and safe place for Sasha to park herself at night.

LIMITATIONS as ROADBLOCKS are very much like that. We will all agree, that, while we don't like staring at this rock in the road, there is something oddly comfortable about it, and we'll move ahead, only when we are good and ready. A LIMITATION is like being in the kitty litter boxes of our lives, to stretch a metaphor way further than you thought I would. When your life is "stinky" enough, you will probably ask yourself, could this be my litter box? and, "Why?" "What am I getting out of this LIMITATION that keeps me in such a disagreeable situation?" "What is the proverbial 'payoff' for my self-destructive behavior?"

A common LIMITATION is found in the old adage, "Hitch your wagon to a star!" While, with Hollywood's celluloid interpretations may seem innocuous enough, this adage conjures up images of guys and dolls, a knight in shining armor, an ecstatic couple riding into the sunset—a happy ending—and the screen goes black with "THE END."

In real life, at this point, real people get up from their theater seats, find their ways to the exits, where they toss their popcorn sacks and paper cups, and where they fumble for their car keys as their eyes adjust to the lights of the real world. Still, many of us, as though mesmerized by a steady diet of video, television, radio and film, actually leave the collective theaters of our lives and carry with us the post-hypnotic suggestion that the equation for "happily ever after" includes "hitch your wagon to a star," rather than authoring the script of our life ourselves. We believe that we need someone or something outside of ourselves to be happy, to be whole. Unaware, we assume a dependent and needy role in our lives, and we unwittingly abdicate the role of producer, director and leading lady or man in our own autobiographical masterpiece.

Stereotypically, the majority of individuals seeking their fortune and future bliss by finding their "stars" are women, who have grown up believing that walking into that sunset with the right guy is just the beginning of Heaven on earth. Of course, we all know, the sunset is a painted movie set, and the "right guy" is more than likely searching for the "right gal" to ensure his eternal happiness. One thing I know for certain, having plenty of "insider information" from years of listening to both men and women explore their dreams and their emptiness, is that to "hitch your wagon to a star" is a surefire way to guarantee that you will not ever have the exhilarating experience of becoming a star yourself.

If you have ever sat across from a therapist who has confronted you with the fact that you seem surprisingly eager to please others ahead of yourself, to move mountains to discover what they want from you, rather than asking yourself what you want, you probably know how "clueless" really feels. If you are fortunate, your therapist will pose the question bluntly, "So, what exactly is the payoff for putting yourself last?" (Usually, here, the therapist's credentials are quickly scanned in the client's mind and he or she suddenly doesn't seem so omniscient and caring as before.) When we are stalled out or crushed by the ROADBLOCK of LIMITATION, as with any other ROADBLOCK, there is a payoff even if we are unaware of what it might be.

LIMITATIONS as a ROADBLOCK came for me in the form of perfectionism. While I had confidence that I could make it okay socially wherever I went, I felt that in all things considered a formal achievement, things like school, art, music, dance or writing a book, somehow I had to do it perfectly, or it would be a disaster. This perfectionism was definitely reinforced when I took piano lessons from a first generation German piano teacher who shouted out the rhythm and rapped my knuckles with a ruler when I missed a note. I remember arriving each week for my lesson, timid and nervous inside. As I waited for my turn, I listened to the last strains of works by Chopin and Beethoven played boldly and brilliantly by Jeanine Kretschmer, the valedictorian in my high school class and a virtuoso on the piano. Jeanine was perfect. I was not. To this day I can play the first five bars of Chopin's Concerto in F Flat Major, and nothing else. I obsessed over this tiny portion of a classical work far beyond my abilities, and never learned to play the piano just for fun. This is a LIMITATION, believing that I had to be far more skilled at the piano than I was. Or else!

Perfectionism. It's a ROADBLOCK of LIMITATION that will stop the best of us. Shel Silverstein sums it up in this verse:

Almost Perfect

'Almost perfect . . .but not quite,'
Those were the words of Mary Hume
At her seventh birthday party,
Looking 'round the ribboned room.

'This tablecloth is pink not white—
Almost perfect, but not quite.'

'Almost perfect . . . but not quite,'
Those were the words of grown-up Mary
Talking about her handsome beau,
The one she wasn't gonna marry.
Squeezes me a bit too tight—
Almost perfect . . . but not quite.'

'Almost perfect . . . but not quite,'
Those were the words of ol' Miss Hume
Teaching in the seventh grade,
Grading papers in the gloom.
'They never cross their 'T's' just right—
Almost perfect . . . but not quite.'

Ninety-eight the day she died,
Complainin' 'bout the spotless floor.
People shook their heads and sighed,
'Guess that she'll like heaven more.'
Up went her soul on feathered wings.
Out the door, up out of sight.
Another voice from heaven came—
'Almost perfect . . . but not quite.'

Procrastination is one of the tip-offs that we are facing a ROADBLOCK of LIMITATION. I remember several years ago when I was supervising the clinical work of a Ph.D. candidate and she was at the crucial stage in her studies of writing her dissertation. One day in the office I noticed that the kitchen pantry was particularly orderly, in fact, the soups and spices had been arranged alphabetically! I commented to the office manager that, while this was really quite delightful, it was far beyond her job description. She told

110

me that she hadn't done it. Yep, that's right. It was the doctoral candidate! Caught in the clutches of procrastination, she was cleaning everything in sight. She too finally burst through her ROADBLOCK of LIMITATION and has been a successful licensed psychologist for many years now with a thriving private practice of her own.

Somehow, the ROADBLOCK of LIMITATION seems to affect us in very idiosyncratic and unpredictable ways. For me, the writing of this book was delayed at least ten years due to my unrealistic idea of how phenomenal it just had to be in order to pass muster. Chalk this up to too many courses in literary criticism or sheer egocentrism gone insecure; I have had writer's block beyond my understanding. Then, finally, the statute of limitations on my LIMITATION was magically up, and now it seems that nothing can keep me from the keyboard. I am ready to go. I am writing it for myself and having the time of my life!

LIMITATIONS are often ROADBLOCKS when we stifle our creativity and suffer the pangs of self-consciousness, as though the world were watching. Our childlike egocentricity misleads us into believing that we are actually the center of the universe, just as Ptolemy postulated that the earth was at the center of the solar system. Once we make the paradigm shift in self-perception, we forever alter our relationship with reality, just as Copernicus did for astronomy when he centered the sun among the planets. LIMITATIONS of self-consciousness are shattered by the German philosopher Heidegger who wrote of the non-local mind, "A person is neither a thing nor a process, but an opening or clearing through which the Absolute can manifest."

By definition, LIMITATIONS are self-imposed and generated by our emotional nature. Fueled by fear, they often fly in the face of the true and the factual. For example, in my private practice I have worked with young men who were as good looking as Tom Cruise or Kevin Costner, yet so shy they couldn't bring themselves to go on a date. Their LIMITATION ROADBLOCK had to do with feeling insecure with women, feeling they would embarrass themselves enormously and the paralysis that comes with such thoughts. Fortunately, for them also, at some point in time, they were "done" with this particular ROADBLOCK, began dating, and, years later, have sent me smiling photographs of their beautiful new wives and children.

Some people never quite make it past their LIMITATIONS of the fear of striking out and risking getting their feelings hurt in relationships. They choose (by default) a life alone, safe from the inevitable heartbreak and loss that accompanies great joy and love. One of my favorite little verses by C.C. Mitchell helps us take this lightly:

> *Here lie the bones of Old Miss Jones*
> *For her, life held no terrors.*
> *She lived an old maid*
> *She died an old maid,*
> *No hits, no runs, no errors.*

LIMITATION as a ROADBLOCK can halt one's forward progress, detour a person from pursuing a career or avocation for which they are actually meant. In short, LIMITATION is a ROADBLOCK that you don't ever want in your way. Usually, when I'm working with a client staring at his own ROADBLOCK of LIMITATION, he can talk his way around it, complain to me why it is illogical, advise his friends and colleagues against falling prey to the same ROADBLOCK, yet not be able to remove it himself, despite all his IQ points or compelling reasoning. This is because our LIMITATION

ROADBLOCKS are emotional in nature, not rational. The longest distance between two points seems to be the eighteen inches between the neo-cortex and the heart, between one's thinking and one's feeling. This is the therapist's challenge— to help the client traverse this expanse in order to remove the ROADBLOCKS that stand in the way. When we are stopped by self-imposed LIMITATION, we need perspective to help us overcome it. This perspective must be charged with emotion, because our LIMITATION, like all our other ROADBLOCKS, has become a habit and habits resist reason and defy logic. Horace Mann wrote of the tyranny of habits in his statement, "Habits are like a cable. We weave a strand of it everyday and soon it cannot be broken." And Aristotle himself opined, "We are what we repeatedly do."

For most of us, the frustration of being kept from reaching one's goals eventually becomes so painful that it helps us overcome the fear of failure. The pain of leaving our comfort zone eventually becomes less than that of living a life unlived. When that finally occurs, we challenge the LIMITATION that has stubbornly separated us from our dreams, and begin to remove it from our path.

After all, intrinsic motivation is, in fact, teleological in nature. That is to say, our aspirations and inspirations have to do with our purpose, what we were designed to be in the master plan in which we are each playing a part. In the words of Lloyd C. Douglas, "We are not pushed from behind, but magnetized from beyond." In the case of facing the ROADBLOCK of LIMITATION, our greatest tool is our own personal and powerful emotions. It is an inescapable fact that we are all co-creators of our own realities. Each of us is so much more than we realize, that when we plow headlong into a LIMITATION, we experience a feeling of being diminished, of shrinking from our true purpose in life. Yet, we are not cattle, trained to stay within the corral. We are so much more. Nikos Kazantzakis wrote in *Zorba the Greek*, "What a strange machine man is? You fill him with bread, wine, fish and radishes, and out of him come sighs, laughter and dreams." He called us "dream machines" and said, "A dream is a wish your heart makes."

Usually when we are stopped by LIMITATIONS we are feeling an odd melange of inadequacy, perfectionism, unworthiness, fear of failure, and extreme egocentrism. Interesting, isn't it, that egocentrism is really an irrational self-consciousness, the delusion that other people are paying particular attention to what we are doing. This distorted notion is extremely limiting and far from true, because after all, since it is human nature to be egocentric, it follows that the other six-plus billion people on the planet are fully occupied with self-centered considerations themselves and few, if any have extra time to be thinking about you and me! It was Pir Vilayat Khan who summed it up very well in his statement, "The assumption of being an *individual* is our greatest LIMITATION."

Needless to say, a therapist sees clients daily who struggle with calamitous situations, tragedies, disappointment, loss and grief—all apparent LIMITATIONS. Adjusting to the unexpected pitfalls in life is sometimes almost more than we can bear. At times like this, most of us just want to feel connected to another soul who will be with us in our pain. It takes superb timing to know just when to encourage a person who has suffered a loss. Yet, we risk stalling out behind the ROADBLOCK of LIMITATION if we stay too long in our sorrow. It was Helen Keller who wrote, "When one door of happiness closes another opens, but often we look so long at the closed door that we do not see the one which has been opened for us." Helen Keller, the visionary, shows us the truth about the limits of LIMITATIONS, despite being born without the gifts of sight or hearing.

History is filled with examples of people who finally faced their ROADBLOCKS of LIMITATION and moved along to achieve great things. Napoleon Hill once asked Henry Ford where ideas come from. There was something like a saucer on the desk in front of Ford. He flipped it upside down, tapped the bottom with his fingers and said, "You know that atmospheric pressure is hitting this object at fourteen pounds per square inch. You can't see it or feel it but you know it is happening. It's that way with ideas. The air is full of them. They are knocking you on the head. You only have to know what you want, then forget it and go about your business. Suddenly the idea you want will come through. It was there all the time."

Most inspirational literature, it seems, tells the stories of individuals that rose to greatness, people who have become famous for their extraordinary gifts and talents, or for their achievement of extraordinary feats. Ironically, while we may be deeply touched by the truths they offer us, we may also feel oddly separated from them, reasoning that we are somehow essentially different, and that their stories, even the morals of their stories, couldn't actually apply to us. We reason, through LIMITATION, that we are less significant, our lives less interesting, less meaningful. Yet, if we dare accept the concept of the non-local mind, the possibility that we are each part of an infinite whole, rather than separate and individual, we are free to reach beyond our perceived LIMITATIONS and into the realms of infinite possibilities. In short, we are able to transmute our weaknesses into our strengths, just as Helen Keller turned her lack of physical sight into perpetual vision.

Each of us has a simple story to tell of how we turned our LIMITATIONS into our strengths. I remember during the years I was growing up in the home of a career Air Force officer's family and moving from place to place every few years, the necessity of learning how to fit in, gain friends quickly and become included in the local school and neighborhood. As I proceeded through schools from New York to Virginia to Alabama to Alaska, to New Mexico, to Missouri and finally Arkansas, Alaska, Spain and Texas, at the top of the priorities with each move was to land on my feet socially and academically, and fully experience the magic of each of those wonderful locales.

I might have interpreted this nomadic lifestyle as being filled with LIMITATIONS and loss, as, in fact, my friends did seem to vanish every few years and life was like a conveyor belt of new scenery, climates, school buildings and classmates. Instead, my parents ensured that my sisters and I experienced our lifestyle as our family's grand adventure, and we took every opportunity to make each "transfer" to a new Air Force Base a vacation via the likes of Disneyland, The Grand Canyon, or Pikes Peak. My parents helped me experience change with anticipation and delight, rather than resistance and regret. They helped me learn how to determine my own response to outer circumstances, rather than settle for the helplessness of LIMITATION.

Needless to say, this experience of traveling the world broadened my horizons and offered me ways to gain confidence and understanding of the diversity of values and cultures of a multitude of different groups of people. This opportunity to become a part of neighborhoods throughout this country and abroad helped me lift my ROADBLOCK of LIMITATIONS in a variety of ways. There is a kind of faith in the goodness of people and the beauty of the planet that comes with this background. Everywhere I went I felt a connectedness among the people I met, and, despite the racial or ethnic differences that may have separated me from others, there was always a common spirit weaving among everyone I met. I learned that my needs and aspirations were fundamentally the same as those of people who didn't even resemble me in many other ways. I learned that we are more alike than we are different. Perhaps, that is what really pulled me back from Arts and Sciences into the applied field of psychology.

If this discussion has sparked your curiosity and you are asking yourself, "Just what is the nature of my ROADBLOCKS of LIMITATIONS, you might ask yourself the simple question, "What would I do if I knew I could not fail?" At first, it is normal to draw a blank and to feel somewhat stunned by the question. After all, this is what you might call a "blue sky" exercise, the kind of brainstorming that large corporations do in think tanks, the precursor to most of our technological breakthroughs and leading edge inventions.

As we move forward, identifying and removing the ROADBLOCKS in our path, we are, in fact, reinventing ourselves. We are all in the business of personal development and transformation. We are exploring the universe that is within ourselves to find great treasure. Once we recognize our ROADBLOCK of LIMITATION we usually find, that, like all the other ROADBLOCKS, this one is an aggregate of many, many experiences and feelings collected through the years. Just as complex and burdensome as concrete, ROADBLOCKS can be broken apart into manageable pieces and tossed into the ditches along the road.

 **is for
OVERFUNCTIONING**

*"What lies behind us and what
lies before us are tiny matters
compared to what lies within us."*

Oliver Wendell Holmes

is for OVERFUNCTIONING. The second "O" of our ROADBLOCKS is one of my very favorites, as I think everyone of you will relate to it. "O" stands for OVERFUNCTIONING. You might think of it in terms of "the need for speed," our preoccupation with being busy, marked by excess in all its dizzying varieties. It might be seen as the "Martha Stewart Syndrome," the need to punctuate every occasion with a greeting card or a social gathering, to let holidays dictate your home décor or even your clothing. OVERFUNCTIONING is a ROADBLOCK in so far as it blinds us to the big picture; it is a kind of myopic approach to life that often leads us straight into the ditch.

Perhaps one of the most effective and eloquent authors in exposing our penchant as a culture for OVERFUNC-TIONING is Anne Wilson Schaef, Ph.D. Dr. Schaef expounds brilliantly on the distressing, in fact "dis-eased" nature of OVERFUNCTIONING from a systems and societal perspective in her earlier books, *When Society Becomes an Addict* and *The Addictive Organization*. However, it was her tiny, pocket-sized book, *Meditations for Women Who Do Too Much* that has reached millions of both women and men and sparked a new cultural awareness of the power we harness when we remove the ROADBLOCK of OVERFUNC-TIONING.

In times past, when we were still in the hunter—gatherer stage of survival as a species, being ever vigilant and industrious was a crucial trait that helped the "fittest" survive. Even in more modern times, during the infancy of this nation

119

and others, an unrelenting work ethic separated those who lived to procreate from those who perished. It was an early Texas woman pioneer who was quoted as saying, "When we rest, we rust." That was an apt motto for the rugged settlers of yesteryear who, from dawn until dusk had to chop wood and carry water. But for those of us in our air-conditioned, twenty-first century worlds, in which much of our time is spent in front of a computer screen or driving an automobile, overwork is a formula for hypertension, addiction, and burnout. Now we "hunt" for clothing and food in shopping malls and on the Internet, and we "gather" mostly information as our source of sustenance. Our time challenges and physical energy expenditures have changed dramatically in the past hundred years. And with this drastic change, a new motto prevails, "use it or lose it."

Adaptation to the Information Age includes the realization that balanced living is most likely to increase both our longevity and quality of life. We now look at Abraham Maslow's hierarchy of needs and realize that all areas of our lives require our attention in order that we feel fulfilled, or in Maslow's term, "self-actualized. No longer required to function on the survival level of centuries past, we now implement the principles of balance and moderation, the mantras of the likes of Deepak Chopra, Marianne Williamson, Tony Robbins, and Melody Beattie. Personal power involves, not the OVERFUNCTIONING of ages past, but the peace of mind that comes when we honor all aspects of our lives, the emotional, spiritual, mental and physical.

"When we rest, we rust" is now an anachronism, an OLD IDEA that has led to OVERFUNCTIONING. Once adaptive, it is now maladaptive, and updating it to overcome OVERFUNCTIONING can feel counterintuitive, as we have counted on it for thousands, maybe millions of years, just to stay alive. Reprogramming our internal messages can be extremely difficult, simply because of our history and years of absolute reliance on the outdated message for survival. Typically, when something is as deeply ingrained as a survival mechanism, rather than transforming and truly upgrading to appropriate era-appropriate activities, most people merely cross-addict to a new version of the old message. In this case, and as we will discuss in this chapter, most of us merely cross-addict to OVERFUNCTIONING.

One OVERFUNCTIONING client of mine presented with anxiety and depression related, not to biochemical imbalance, but to her need to succeed. With three small children and a workaholic executive husband, she defined herself by her ZIP code, her position in the Junior League and the theme clothing she wore (Halloween sweaters with flashing orange and black lights, Christmas socks that chimed Christmas carols when she walked, earrings to go with every event). Why, it made me tired just seeing her name on my schedule each week!

OVERFUNCTIONING is greatly encouraged by the weekend warrior shows on television, retail merchandising and a thousand other ways. We see role models of OVERFUNCTIONING moms and dads smiling up at us from the magazines on our coffee tables. Fathers are shown building garden furniture, tree houses and remodeling perfectly fine kitchens. Mothers are shown faux-finishing walls, gluing buttons onto lampshades, turning the nursery into theme parks, with handmade drapes and hand-stenciled flooring. Observing holidays has been elevated to an art form and we now have Easter Egg Trees, Valentine's clothing, Halloween lighting, not to mention New Year's Eve hysteria. And this is just the holidays! We see OVERFUNCTIONING on Wall Street, in the workplace as well as on the home front.

With our global economy and the Internet, we now have offices in our homes, even offices in our automobiles and some of us take Barbara Walters' television directive, "We're in touch, so you be in touch," far too literally. OVERFUNCTIONING appears to be one ROADBLOCK with something for everyone—a ROADBLOCK that requires skill to identify and eliminate.

Shel Silverstein sums up the feeling one has when good efforts and the best of intentions get out of hand and become OVERFUNCTIONING in this very clever verse, "Tired" from *Where the Sidewalk Ends*:

> *I've been working so hard you just wouldn't believe,*
> *And I'm tired!*
> *There's so little time and so much to achieve,*
> *And I'm tired!*
> *I've been lying here holding the grass in its place.*
> *Pressing a leaf with the side of my face.*
> *Tasting the apples to see if they're sweet,*
> *Counting the toes on a centipede's feet.*
> *I've been memorizing the shape of that cloud,*
> *Warning the robins to not chirp so loud,*
> *Shooing the butterflies off the tomatoes,*
> *Keeping an eye out for floods and tornadoes.*
> *I've been supervising the work of the ants*
> *And thinking of pruning the cantaloupe plants,*
> *Timing the sun to see what time it sets,*
> *Calling the fish to swim into my nets,*
> *And I've taken twelve thousand and forty-one breaths,*
> *And I'm TIRED!*

A society that once had mothers who stayed at home to give birth and raise young children, now has them returning home from the hospital within 24-48 hours of giving birth, despite the scientific fact that post-partum depression is a universal and serious medical phenomenon, and that without treatment it can present life-threatening risks to both mother and child alike. What was once revered as a sacred event and accommodated within the family as an unchallenged first priority, one worthy of a whole extended family network of support, is now trivialized and relegated to just another day, another opportunity to OVERFUNCTION.

By OVERFUNCTIONING, we seize onto life's most transforming events, such as the birth of a child, and trivialize them into "photo opportunities." We waste our energy on the frills of printing the blessed announcement in the local newspaper and finding a clever way to announce the Hallmark moment to our friends. By losing track of the natural bonding of mother and child, and the importance of building a foundation for a lifetime, we focus instead on the superficial, quickly sending new mothers back to the office, while women's magazines encourage them to "have it all!" Gone are the "lazy, hazy, crazy days of summer" that some of us remember as children, and here to stay are soccer and football camps, trips to stay a month with Dad (or Mom), summer school and a myriad of lessons, classes or must-do events for kids. Our children practically require Day Timers, or Palm Pilots of their own to juggle their over-scheduled little lives, and their parents have become their sleep-deprived chauffeurs. OVERFUNCTIONING results in overlooking the priceless value of childhood and building memories the old fashioned way, by living them.

Our families are becoming as processed as our food, with more and more instruction coming from television or computer software instead of story telling, skinned knees and Sunday school. The consequences of this social upheaval of priorities are immeasurable. Despite the cost in lost quality time, eroding values and human suffering, we remain puzzled, even mystified about the impact the "do it all" mentality is having on us as a society. Even though the evidence of this fast-forward lifestyle blares at us nightly on the network news, we persist, and allow ourselves to be mesmerized by the media's nightly documentaries on tragedies related to suicide, homicide, and other stress-related horrors. We watch the nightly coverage of school violence or some civil servant "going postal" as though we were watching fiction, deriving some form of voyeuristic pleasure from the stimulation of it all. Almost as if in the aftermath of a kind of collective Posttraumatic Stress Disorder, we are numbed to the reality of it, and robotic-like, we do it all over again tomorrow.

It seems clear that in this society we have settled for quantity over quality and that in our pursuit of the American Dream have created the American Nightmare. While we crave emotional and spiritual fulfillment, we settle for a collective trance in which we ask life to imitate not necessarily art, but make-believe. We look to television, the silver screen, sports courts and venues of all kinds for inspiration and entertainment. Day-by-day, we find ourselves captivated by the headlines or the stock market, and day-by-day, we let another opportunity go by to be a player, to take a chance, to live as though it mattered. Rather than making a difference, many of us confuse appearance with substance and busy ourselves building our wardrobe, remodeling our house or expanding our portfolio. Emerson noticed this phenomenon of OVERFUNCTIONING as early as the 19th century as he observed, "We are always getting ready to live, but never living."

During the past several years we have learned much about OVERFUNCTONING from the recovery movements of

Twelve Step programs. By now, it is common knowledge that every addict requires an enabler; every person caught in the throes of workaholism, alcoholism or any other "ism" who is medicating feelings with too much of "a good thing" requires a codependent, a person whose job it is to caretake, to OVERFUNCTION in order to free up the addict to keep on practicing his or her addiction.

In the case of substance abuse, this is easily seen. The enabler, the codependent, loses sight of his or her inner reality as she becomes fixated on the addict's reality and OVERFUNCTIONS to support the addict's lifestyle. In the much more common and subtle instances of the workaholic and the appendage-like partner, the codependent OVERFUNCTIONER, the scene looks a lot like a regular television commercial for a minivan or a sport utility vehicle. Usually, the OVERFUNCTIONING, glamorous (supermodel) wife and mother of four is merrily shuttling children from violin lessons to soccer, doing grocery shopping and grooming the family pet, all in a day's work. This OVERFUNCTIONER appears to be the perfect "soccer mom" so wooed and schmoozed by our politicians that she has been elevated to an almost icon-like stature in our society. Meanwhile, back at the office, it is usually the male who is portrayed as a dapper stock market-watching, GQ kind of a guy, working late in some high-rise to "bring home the bacon" after a 60-80 hour week. The alter ego of this city slicker workaholic partner to our OVERFUNCTIONER is sometimes merely a pot-bellied Bubba character in a recliner with a six-pack watching Monday night football with his buddies.

The most insidious form of OVERFUNCITONING in my opinion just may be the everyday kind of codependency rather than the codependency that enables alcohol and other drug abuse. This garden variety of OVERFUNCTIONING is seen when an individual is clearly missing the big picture, busying oneself with trivia, the "gimme's" of life, the jobs that are never really finished, like the dishes or the laundry. When one "key holes" the detailing of one's automobile, wardrobe and home, investing excessive time and emphasis on the outer appearances of things while neglecting one's inner development and emotional, mental and spiritual growth, one is probably involved in OVERFUNCTIONING. The challenge of identifying this ROADBLOCK is apparent. The OVERFUNCTIONING individual's activities are so appreciated by others, samples of which are featured in "House Beautiful" or "Town and Country" and other eye-candy publications, that one is usually well-regarded for practicing this ROADBLOCK. The rewards are often merely the accolades from a dinner guest or the reputation in the neighborhood or carpool as being "a really nice person."

Heavily invested in people-pleasing, the OVERFUNC-TIONING person settles for a role dependent on the approval of other people, a role re-written daily by the changing demands of those she is committed to "making happy." When faced with this black hole of a ROADBLOCK, one's work is never done and one's motto is, "God is in the details."

The OVERFUNCTIONING individual pays "the price of nice" (to use Robert Bolton's brilliant phrase) and sacrifices a self-directed life in order to serve as the support staff for others. After years of preparing meals, redecorating the already lovely home, re-organizing the contents of the pantry or keeping track daily of family finances on the home computer, feelings of resentment, and anger accumulate so gradually that when they explode (or implode, as they usually do) they seem to appear from out of nowhere! The "price of nice" includes not only addictive disorders, psychosomatic disorders, but also depression, anxiety and, not uncommonly, the dissolution of marriages and the fracturing of families. OVERFUNCTIONING might aptly be considered a killer ROADBLOCK wearing an apron and a smile.

OVERFUNCTIONING like everything else is measured on a continuum. The litmus test of whether one's attention to detail and minutia is, actually OVERFUNCTIONING, or merely an expression of one's creativity and love of life is quite simple. Simply ask yourself, "Am I acting out of love or out of fear?" The question is quite basic, "Are my daily activities flowing from my enthusiasm and joy of living? Am I feeling expansive and engaged, knowing that I make a positive difference on the planet? Or do I move from one task to the next, feeling fatigued, hassled and resentful that no one else ever cares enough to make the bed, pick up the clutter, wash the dog or ask me how my day was?

When one is OVERFUNCTIONING there is a mechanical aspect to one's consciousness. In fact, when one is faced with this ROADBLOCK, one typically feels put upon, diminished, burdened and bored. The OVERFUNC-TIONING individual may whistle while she works, but inevitably exudes an air of the victim, and is usually quite indirect about communicating this to others. The clues are often subtle, and may be seen in one's facial expression, one's posture, and a characteristic sigh or verbally through sarcasm, exposing her envy of other people's lives. The tip-off for recognizing OVERFUNCTIONING is the distinct absence of real love and joy.

A great number of my clients throughout the years have presented with symptoms of depression, burnout, disillusionment, marital problems and other complaints related to their respective lifestyles of OVERFUNC-

TIONING. Once they begin to peel back layers of confusion, guilt about finally seeking help for themselves, and start to discover that they have repressed considerable resentment and anger towards those for whom they have cared so faithfully for so long, they frequently object to the possibility that perhaps, in Robin Norwood's words, they might be people "Who love too much." Another term for this OVERFUNCTIONING of course is "codependency."

Typically the hypothesis of "loving too much" is rejected outright with the protestation, "But isn't that the loving thing to do?" And, of course, there's always the follow up, "But isn't it selfish of me to spend time taking care of myself, rather than taking care of everyone else?" To these objections I respond that the answer to their questions lies within them. It is easily discerned by asking whether they are acting from a position of real love or from a sense of obligation or people pleasing, whether they are acting with passion and enthusiasm, or from avoidance of one's own issues. It is the purity of intent that is the key to a loving deed, not the deed itself.

For me, the Bible says it best in "I Corinthians 13":

Though I speak with the tongues of men and of angels and have not love, I am become as sounding brass or a tinkling cymbal. And though I have the gift of prophecy, and understand all mysteries, and all knowledge, and though I have all faith, so that I could remove mountains, and have not love, I am nothing. And though I bestow all my goods to feed the poor, and though I give my body to be burned, and have not love it profiteth me nothing. Love suffereth long and is kind, love envieth not; love

vaunteth not itself, is not puffed up, Doth not behave itself unseemly, seeketh not her own, is not easily provoked, thinketh no evil, rejoiceth not in iniquity but rejoiceth in the truth. Beareth all things, Believeth all things, Endureth all things. Love never faileth.

The ROADBLOCK of OVERFUNCTIONING is actually a form of DENIAL. OVERFUNCTIONING allows one to put out of mind the nagging feelings, issues, or problems that might be painful or unpleasant, but that require our attention if we are to develop personally and spiritually. OVERFUNCTIONING, no matter what flavor, involves focus outside of oneself, and frequently the adoption of a focus on another's problems, and the role of becoming the fixer, the caretaker, the "Mommy" to other adults, as well as to children.

Of course, when we are OVERFUNCTIONING we feel quite entitled, even obligated to continue in our role, as we believe that without our "help" other people might never get it right. Losing sight of the fact that our ultimate obligation as parents is to encourage self-responsibility, we are often OVERFUNTIONING and codependent parents. Since this "helping disease" comes so naturally to us, we often infantalize our spouse as well as our children while we're at it with care-taking condescension. We are usually in complete DENIAL regarding the fact that not only does our "helpfulness" drive our family crazy, but that it is a ROADBLOCK to individual maturity and happiness.

OVERFUNCTIONING may be the most obstinate of ROADBLOCKS, the most difficult to identify and to remove. Usually, the individual plagued by the disease to please, the need to control another's actions, to anticipate and avoid any potential conflict, is actually functioning from an emotional age younger than twelve, and perceiving persons around him as having the capacity to abandon him, reject him or harm him with anger or indifference. The typical OVERFUNCTIONING person uses this ROADBLOCK as a defense mechanism to ward off conflict, either internal or external. The typical OVERFUNCTIONER is driven by fear of emotional unrest and the unresolved issues that lie within, in short, by emotional illiteracy.

This ROADBLOCK like all others is merely a habit that has outworn its usefulness. What may have worked for us at ages four or six or ten, simply begins to backfire when we're twenty-five, forty-seven or eighty-five. By the time we are into our late twenties or early thirties, operating from the outside in the way an OVERFUNCTIONER does becomes a futile exercise in trying to read others' minds, feel their feelings, gauge their reactions. It doesn't take long for us to gradually lose touch with our own opinions, preferences, and selves. The OVERFUNCTIONER plays it safe, always trying to secure the desired outcome. The OVERFUNCTIONER tests the direction of the wind before making each decision, takes a poll before taking a stand. Before too long, the OVERFUNCTIONER loses touch with him or herself, and feels more like a hollow shell, a reflection of someone else's life. She is always "in relation to" as in someone's mother, sister, lover, wife, neighbor, boss or secretary, and never secure with an identity as a separate and complete individual.

Many of the people I see professionally display this OVERFUNCTIONING trait early in their therapy experience. They struggle with the right thing to say to someone or the right way to say it. They agonize over decisions such as whether to turn down a dinner invitation or a date, fearing that they'll hurt someone's feelings. They struggle with the sheer act of telling the truth about what they want and need. When a person is OVERFUNC-TIONING, he is committed to manipulating the outcome, rather than the truth. I am fond of reminding them of the wisdom of television's Davy Crockett played by Fess Parker, who said wryly, "First, be sure you're right; then go ahead." To the OVERFUNCTIONER this requires knowing the truth about what you want and need, and then having the gumption to speak the truth and let go of the consequences.

To anyone who has lived with a raging parent or spouse or child, to anyone who fears physical or verbal abuse, indifference, abandonment or rejection, Davy Crockett's advice goes down like a bitter pill. It is almost impossible to swallow. We simply do not feel that we have the courage.

The key to removing this ROADBLOCK is captured in the phrase, "Letting Go," and here, in verse by an unknown author, is what "letting go" really means:

> *To 'let go' does not mean to stop caring;*
> *It means I can't do it for someone else.*
> *To 'let go' is not to cut myself off,*
> *It's the realization I can't control another.*
> *To 'let go" is not to enable,*
> *But to allow learning from natural consequences.*
> *To 'let go' is to admit powerlessness,*
> *Which means the outcome is not in my hands.*
> *To 'let go' is not to try to change or blame another;*
> *It's to make the most of myself.*
> *To 'let go' is not to care for, but to care about.*
> *To 'let go' is not to fix, but to be supportive.*
> *To 'let go' is not to judge,*
> *But to allow another to be a human being.*

To 'let go' is not to be in the middle of arranging all the
Outcomes, but to allow others to affect their own destinies.
To 'let go' is not to be protective;
It's to permit another to face reality.
To 'let go' is not to deny, but to accept.
To 'let go' is not to nag, scold, or argue, but instead
To search out my own shortcomings and correct them.
To 'let go' is not to adjust everything to my desires but to
Take each day as it comes, and cherish myself in it.
To 'let go' is not to regret the past,
But to grow and live for the future.

To 'let go' is to fear less and love more.

But no matter how ludicrous the illustrations, how comic the portrayal of the OVERFUNCTIONING codependent, now matter how often we laugh at ourselves in cartoons or giggle at the nonsensical busybody characters on sit-coms, most of us are just about as affixed to our habits of OVERFUNCTIONING as if we were attached to them by Velcro or superglue. Why is it so difficult to stop playing God and just mind our own business?

Possibly it involves the fact that to "let go" of another's business and tend to our own involves trust and humility—the admission that we are powerless, and the fact that we must face our plight in the universe ourselves. Considering the spiritual aspects of life, not the ritualized or necessarily religious aspects, but the undeniable fact that we don't understand exactly why we were put on the planet, what our purpose is and what it's all about, is frightening. We avoid considering this at all costs.

Sometimes we avoid facing our spirituality by OVERFUNCTIONING even through religion! We can maximize our church attendance, teach Sunday school, tithe, and volunteer to help others and effectively never have the quiet time we need to get in touch with our feelings, our inner reality, our soul.

Letting go involves trusting a Higher Power. No matter how spiritual we may consider ourselves, letting go is often quite easy to counterfeit, but difficult to do. Most of us pay lip service to a belief in some form of a Supreme Being, Creator, Higher Power, God. Regardless of our religious upbringing or lack of it, most of us know that we did not create ourselves. Nonetheless, we will OVERFUNCTION as though we are, ourselves, in charge of everything. When we learn to "let go" we replace the Texas pioneer woman's phrase, "When we rest, we rust" with "When we rest, we trust."

One wintry day in the mountains of Quebec at a renewal center I had attended and where I was now consulting, I came upon the following verse taped up on the refrigerator. This verse has helped me over the years remove my ROADBLOCK of OVERFUNCTIONING and discover the key to living with faith.

On Letting Go and Trusting God

As children bring their broken toys with
Tears for us to mend.
I brought my broken dreams to God,
Because He was my friend.
But then instead of leaving Him in peace
To work alone,
I hung around and tried to help.
With ways that were my own.
At last I snatched them back and cried,
'How can You be so slow?'
'My child, He said, what could I do?
You never did let go.'

Here are some guidelines for those of us who make OVERFUNCTIONING a way of life. Since OVERFUNC-TIONING leads to burnout and also to the loss of one's inner reality as one becomes addicted to outer reality, the following guidelines are lifesavers, a list we might call the "Codependent's Bill of Rights":

1. *You are important as an individual and you don't have to devote all your time and energy to other peoples needs.*

2. *You don't have to be perfect all the time.*

3. *Every request doesn't have to be met.*

4. *Learn to say, "No."*

5. *Not everyone is going to approve of you.*

6. *Take care of yourself with the same consciousness as you take care of other people. Treat yourself as if you were a visiting dignitary.*

7. *Delegate. It isn't necessary to do it all yourself.*

8. *Focus first on those you love and on what is really important in your life. Keep your eye on the road.*

9. *Focus on the good, not the flaws, and consider that many crises have very little lasting significance.*

10. *Napping is not a sin. You can nap — that's your 10th commandment.*

The ROADBLOCK of OVERFUNCTIONING is the antithesis of the fact that, in some instances, less is more. I remember in college, while I was in a state of perpetual overdrive, dedicated to achieving everything possible and to performing to capacity, I had the realization one day that I was experiencing priceless peak experiences with such rapidity that I literally did not have the opportunity to savor them fully. It occurred to me then that, maybe, someday, I would slow down long enough to remember each glorious high and to take it all in, allowing each magnificent moment to change me and fill me with gratitude.

I remember, too, how deeply touched I was in college as I read *One Day In The Life of Ivan Denisovich* by Alexander Solzhenitsyn. I empathized with the protagonist, Ivan, a young man in prison who felt overwhelming elation when he was promoted to the position of serving in the food line and was able to have more than one ladle of watered down porridge a day. This shift in his good fortune and this surge of well being was, for Ivan, an epiphany. He realized in an instant, that all our experiences are relative. The less we have had, the more we appreciate and the more intensely we experience the slightest advantage or pleasure. Happiness comes from within.

Since the human being is so easily bored, sated, and numbed, it would seem that we might benefit from lessons in marveling, appreciating, contemplating, rather than continuing to heap more onto our plates. As a culture, it is now a fact statistically that more than 50% of us beyond the age of 25 are seriously overweight, and that's just in pounds and ounces. If we were to measure our "stimulation obesity," I am certain that the statistics would be even more staggering. OVERFUNCTIONING will result in fatigue, boredom and exhaustion, but never in satisfaction or fulfillment. One must ask the obvious, "Why are we going so fast and filling our days to the brim? What's the point?"

The country music group "Alabama" has a terrific song entitled, "I'm in a Hurry and I Don't Know Why." The first stanza makes the point:

> *I'm in a Hurry to get things done,*
> *I rush and rush until life's no fun.*
> *All I've really gotta do is live and die*
> *But I'm in a hurry and I don't know why.*

In this society, the answer seems to be our claim to "Life, liberty and the pursuit of happiness." All this excess, and the OVERFUNCTIONING ROADBLOCK which results, appears to be a sad miscalculation of effort, the proverbial road paved with good intentions, but leading only to a ROADBLOCK.

If we are to identify our own ROADBLOCK of OVERFUNCTIONING we must compare what we experience each day with the question of what happiness really means. We'll have to assess the wisdom of living our life, as we know it. Leo Buscaglia, that lovable, huggable motivational speaker and author, writes of happiness:

> *Happiness is having a sense of self—not a*
> *Feeling of being perfect but of being good enough*
> *And knowing you are in the process of*
> *Growth, of being and achieving levels of joy.*

Eastern cultures cultivate the ability to appreciate beauty in all its forms and elevate this capacity to marvel to become an integral part of their philosophy and spiritual beliefs. We have learned much from these and other societies and, in our own way, have created our own homegrown versions of this skill of marveling, being mindful and conscious of even the tiniest of miracles and wonders. Needless to say, it requires one to slow down in order to magnify the subtlest of wonders and to become mindful. An unknown author wrote: "The miracles of nature do not seem miracles because they are so common. If no one had ever seen a flower, even a dandelion would be the most startling event in the world."

I find in my clinical work that my clients frequently present with symptoms of stress or burnout, and appear to be oblivious to the beauty or magnificence of their own lives. Frequently these patients present with symptoms including fatigue, depression, anxiety, and substance abuse. Whether they have been "self-medicating" their feelings of malaise, futility or other pain with food, alcohol or other drugs, many have been OVERFUNCTIOINING quite innocently, and have not yet realized that fact. Most often, once they begin to look inside, they can admit that they are avoiding something painful, trying not to feel the feelings associated with their fears, and therefore, "medicating" themselves with, not only substances, but also with the art and science of staying too busy, of taking on someone else's life as theirs to manage—in short, with OVERFUNCTIONING.

While we are too busy with the outer reality to feel our own feelings, we lose touch with the ability to marvel, to take in fully the absolute wonder of our lives and of the tiniest of miracles that we experience, but usually overlook, every day. OVERFUNCTIONING literally blinds us to all things present as we find ourselves crucified on the cross between yesterday and tomorrow. OVERFUNCTIONING robs us of the wonders of the world and leaves us empty, unfulfilled. William Blake in his "Auguries of Innocence" clearly describes our proper task:

To see a world in a grain of sand,
And a heaven in a wild flower,
Hold infinity in the palm of your hand,
And eternity in an hour.

I am particularly fond of this whimsical verse by an anonymous poet about being mindful. It challenges us to perfect the art of marveling at even the most everyday and regular things. It takes the ridiculous to new heights, but makes it impossible to miss the point:

Eggomania

Consider the egg. It's a miracle.
A thing so diverse for its size
That we hardly can help growing lyrical
When given the Pullet Surprise!

The scope of this fearless comestible
Must drive other foods to despair.
Since it's not only fully digestible,
But it's great for shampooing the hair!

It's boilable, poachable, fryable,
It scrambles; it makes a sauce thicken.
It's also the only reliable
Device for producing a chicken!

And Helen Lowry Marshall captures the art of appreciating the wonders of the simplest things in life:

The Sacraments of Daily Living

Each day upon my daily round
I find myself on holy ground,
The morning glories on my fence
Inspire quiet reverence.

Just one small, tender seedling grew
And now this miracle in blue.
A robin in the apple tree
Sings out his glad Doxology.

I hear the pure unstifled joy
Of laughter from a little boy.
I bow before the firm belief
And faith of one who lives with grief.

I watch a jet plane skim the skies
And marvel at man's enterprise.
I look upon a field of wheat
And thank God for the bread we eat.

I watch the benedictive rain on
Low bowed heads of flower and grain.
A friend drops in, a neighbor calls,
The lamps are lit, night gently falls.

Contentment settles with the sun
And labor of the day well done,
So many little altars there,
So many simple calls to prayer.

So many reasons for Thanksgiving
The sacraments of daily living.

Restored to living a life fully conscious, awakened to the miracles all about us, and determined to repay the debt of our forefathers by making a difference, we overcome the ROADBLOCK of OVERFUNCTIONING. Rather than overlooking the obligations and opportunities of each day, we recognize distractions, sort out the trivia from the truth and begin to live purposeful lives. We recognize the empty promises of OVERFUNCTIONING, just as though it were a casino rising mirage-like out of the desert. It is tempting in all its glitz and glamour, but we are wise to the odds, and we turn away. Edwin Markham summed up a well-lived life in his verse, "Man Making."

> *We all are blind until we see*
> *That in the human plan*
> *Nothing is worth the making if*
> *It does not make the man.*
>
> *Why build these cities glorious*
> *If man unbuilded goes?*
> *In vain, we build the world, unless*
> *The builder also grows.*

A simple anecdote illustrates the power of attending to ourselves, dedicating ourselves to spiritual, mental, physical and emotional development and greatness. I love to share this with groups to whom I speak, and I frequently close my talks with this simple story:

> *"A father was working one day at home while caring for his three year-old son. To keep his young son occupied, the father cut out a picture of the world from a magazine and made from it a puzzle for his little boy to work on.*

After just a very short time, the man's son called out for his father to come and look. He had already completed the puzzle. The father was quite astonished, as the puzzle had many pieces and the little boy was barely three years old. Surprised and amazed, the father asked with incredulity, "Son, how in the world did you put that together so quickly? Why, you have never even seen a world map before!"

The young boy smiled up at his father with pride and answered, "Oh, it was easy, Dad. On the other side was a picture of a boy. I put the boy together and the world turned out okay!"

 **is for COMPARISON**

*"I don't know the key to
success, but the key to failure
is trying to please everybody."*

Bill Cosby

C is for COMPARISON. The "C" in ROADBLOCKS stands for COMPARISON, a ROADBLOCK when it is accompanied by distorted thinking, and, much to our chagrin, it almost always is. As a therapist, privy to the contrast between personal secrets and public presentations, it is easy to see how we all seem to compare our inner feelings with the outer appearances of others. Put more simply, we usually compare our insides with others' outsides, like comparing apples and oranges. The ROADBLOCK appears when we do not realize we are making this mistake in judgment, and when we are left with feelings that we fall short, by COMPARISON.

To compound the problem further, we all develop this ROADBLOCK of COMPARISON as very young children as we are forming our identities vis a vis the world, our fundamental self-concepts about how we fit into the scheme of things. Dr. Alfred Adler, protégé of Freud and a pioneer in the field of psychiatry, wrote extensively about this natural phenomenon among all humans to develop feelings of both inferiority and superiority through early experiences in relationship with others. Within our families, or in Adler's terminology, "family constellations," we establish some sense of who we are, based on our self-assessment as compared with family members. Adler developed a highly respected personality theory on the importance of birth order to predict personality characteristics that would last a lifetime. He explained how one's earliest years determine the nature of one's self-concept and the resultant feelings of competency, compliance, rebelliousness, creativity and willingness to take risks as well as motivation to succeed.

According to Adler and most developmental psychologists today, to compare oneself with others as a young child is an inevitable part of establishing a healthy identity. This process becomes a ROADBLOCK only when we fail to stop and take stock of how our early self-impressions and expectations unconsciously and adversely influence our choices in life. While our early lessons in self-concept assist us in finding a place among others, our position in the pecking order, if you will, COMPARISON blocks our progress when it is marked by irrationality, automatic and negative self-talk, or magical thinking. COMPARISON may temporarily fuel our ego, but eventually will leave us running on fumes, or out of gas all together, as all faulty COMPARISONS are empty, devoid of lasting value.

COMPARISON blocks our ability to be fully in the moment, enjoying ourselves from within our own skin. COMPARISON results in what I call "pasterizing and futurizing," removing us from the driver's seat and the exhilarating action of the "here and now" moment. COMPARISON drags us backward into the world of regret, the world of "what if's" and "if only's," and results in a life of re-runs of our own lives! COMPARISON also catapults us headlong into apprehension and "anticipointment" about what is yet to come, into mental and emotional rehearsals of our worst fears.

Each of us has an internal photo album of experiences that become ROADBLOCKS to our happiness and success. It's a crazy patchwork piece of perception made of remnants from our family history with all its secrets, scraps from our everyday feelings of uncertainty and the hopes and fears that come with facing the unknown. Some of the patches are made from blue ribbons we won in the swimming tournament or photos of us holding our tennis trophies. Some are fond memories of catching the winning touchdown or being chosen for the Homecoming Court in high school. Just as often the memories will include the darker moments of being left out of a game, not invited to a party, or rejected by someone we cared for. While we usually capture the happier "Kodak moments" on film, frame and display them for all to see, we tend to keep the troubling, sad or guilty memories to ourselves within our internal photo album, where we view them over and over again through the process of "pasterizing."

Take it from someone who ought to know, one's "inside" personal photo album rarely resembles the "outside" that we present for others to see. Most of us reason that to succeed, we have to "have it all together" and I have yet to meet a person who fits that description. We all develop a "false self," a façade that we believe the world will welcome and reward. Of course, it is also just such a façade that others have fashioned for themselves that we see, and sometimes err as we compare it with our internal reality.

Perhaps a glimpse into my own photo album from childhood will make the point. When I was eight years old living in Montgomery, Alabama, the oldest of three children, my thirteen-year-old cousin Martha Jean really captured my attention. She too was an oldest sister, and I remember how pretty she was, how grown up and sophisticated. Martha Jean at thirteen seemed perfect in every way. She was tall and very shapely. Suddenly a teenager, she wore lipstick and seemed to be the paragon of feminine beauty. In all my eight-year-old reasoning, COMPARISON seemed just fine with me. I too wanted to be lovely, shapely, feminine and mature. Instead, I was merely the shortest kid in my class, just a very little girl in the third grade—

no shapely figure, no lipstick, and no way to compete with my blossoming cousin, Martha Jean, who seemed absolutely gorgeous. Somehow, my internal logic concluded, that as the two oldest cousins, I should be just like her, a lovely teenager. COMPARISON was a ROADBLOCK that took up much of that third grade year, as I continually found new ways to try in vain to measure up to Martha Jean.

I remember riding in the back seat of our 1953 Buick measuring my small self against the marvelous Martha Jean and feeling so short compared to her, that I would sit on my knees to make myself appear taller. Then, I would cover my legs with my skirt hoping no one would notice the difference. I remember stretching to my fullest height to catch my reflection in the rear view mirror and check to see if my head was equal in the mirror with Martha Jean's. At the age of eight, I was gauging my self-worth with a "yardstick" that made no sense at all. I reasoned that I had to be as tall as my thirteen year-old cousin was in order to make the grade.

COMPARISON is like highway robbery, as it steals from us the precious gift of the present, and leaves us unfulfilled, unsatisfied and unhappy. I was stunned by the wisdom of a 14 year-old poet named Jason Lehman, about the tragedy of living with this ROADBLOCK:

Present Tense

It was Spring, but it was Summer I wanted;
The warm days, and the great outdoors.
It was Summer, but it was Fall I wanted;
The colorful leaves, and the cool, dry air.
It was Fall, but it was Winter I wanted;
The beautiful snow, and the joy of the Holiday Season.
It was Winter, but it was Spring I wanted;

The warmth, and the blossoming of nature.
I was a child, but it was adulthood I wanted;
The freedom, and the respect.
I was twenty, but it was thirty I wanted;
To be mature, and sophisticated.
I was middle-aged, but it was twenty I wanted;
The youth, and the free spirit.
I was retired, but it was middle age I wanted;
The presence of mind without limitations.
My life was over, but I never got what I wanted.

So all the while, at the glorious age of eight, I might have been enjoying what third graders do and the carefree life of a child living in the lazy suburbs of Montgomery, Alabama. Instead, I was quite obsessed with being something I could not be, specifically, about a foot taller, with the figure of a teenager, more grown up and attracting the attention of high school boys. Self-defeating thinking? Obviously so. But most of you, if you do a painfully honest personal retrospective, can come up with stories very similar to mine and remove your own COMPARISON ROADBLOCKS through awareness.

Later on in life, our "yardsticks" change in nature, but sometimes our feelings of never quite making it, of always falling short (pardon the pun), remain. We become habituated to the experience of feeling limited, and we begin to carry this assumption around within ourselves as a working hypothesis that helps us justify our lives when they seem mediocre. It helps us rationalize the status quo and reify our non-decisions to "settle" rather than to insist on life's peak experiences.

It is quite natural to be deluded by the false COMPARISONS we make unwittingly as we routinely compare apples with oranges. The human façades we see all about us look terrific. We see them only when they are fully dressed, beautifully coiffed and driving the sexy automobiles they have chosen to make a certain impression. Only rarely do we ever see inside to the very human and vulnerable interiors of our friends, neighbors or even relatives. We compare our own feelings of inadequacy, insecurity or fear to the apparent confidence, the look of "having it made" that we see so often in others. That's exactly what they want us to see! Isn't that what we try to show to them too? Hence, apples and oranges, your inside reality to their outside reality. The ROADBLOCK of COMPARISON keeps us spinning our wheels with constant competition, faulty logic and the resultant feelings of futility and even giving up before we really get started.

Most of us have either read of heard of John Malloy's classic bestseller, *Dress for Success*, and dress we do—to the nines! By the time others see us, we have "gift-wrapped" ourselves in order to impress, and, we reason, achieve success! This is a powerful strategy, and a most valuable tool. Unfortunately, all too often we fail to realize that the dapper anchorperson on the six o'clock news is wearing a "uniform," and that packaging is part of the job. Frequently, the folks with the very best packaging have the most to hide, even from themselves. When we recognize the difference between the actual person and their costume, the proverbial book and its cover, then we do just fine. Nevertheless, we are easily confused, as though being lured, even seduced, by the fantastic belief that some people "have it all together" and inevitably we fall short, by COMPARISON.

The problem with this ROADBLOCK is that, whether we come out ahead or behind, ultimately, we lose, because of the distortion built into the process. We will always find someone who appears to be more successful, youthful or beautiful. Sooner or later, if we continue to play this self-defeating game, we will lose. We will grow tired of feeling diminished, and will eventually shrink from our dreams, our goals and settle for feelings of futility and failure.

COMPARISON reaches far beyond the realms of the everyday interpersonal kind. Much of our faulty self-appraisal by COMPARISON relates to persons we will never meet, individuals that we see in the media. Of course, when Warner Brothers or Disney does the packaging, you can be sure that the gift-wrapping is over the top! But rather than recognize the error of COMPARISON, the obvious fact of image manipulation and even body doubles, we really do want to believe in magic. Possibly left over longings from unrequited fairy tales have led us to believe that there are such things as perfection or "overnight success." These people we call "stars" seem to spring, full-blown onto our television screens replete with fan clubs and platinum records or stock portfolios. From rock and roll "phenoms" to cyber geniuses, it seems that every day there's some fresh, usually extremely young face appearing for their 15 minutes of fame. What do we do with this information about instant success stories, divas and heroes? We compare our inner reality with the packaging designed by Madison Avenue or Hollywood.

Women are especially vulnerable to this ROADBLOCK of COMPARISON, as we aspire to the eternal youth and beauty that stares out at us from the magazine covers in the checkout lines at the supermarket, ironically, when we are at our most frazzled, often on the way home from the office and the daycare center, with children in tow and other errands to run. There on the glossy cover of "Vogue" or "Mademoiselle," or "Seventeen" are the flawless faces of the women with whom we foolishly compare ourselves.

But once again, we are doing the apples/oranges thing. I have proof. Not long ago I came across an article that detailed the artwork for a magazine photograph of none other than Michelle Pfeiffer:

DATE: *1 OCTOBER 1990*
CLIENT: *ESQUIRE/T. KOPPEL*
PRODUCT: *MICHELLE PFEIFFER*
DESCRIPTION: *PHOTO TOUCH-UPS FOR*
                   MAGAZINE COVER

Retouching one dye transfer two-piece strip of Michelle Pfeiffer in red dress. Clean up complexion, soften eye lines, soften smile line, add color to lips, trim chin, remove neck lines, soften line under ear lobe, add highlights to earrings, add blush to cheek, clean up neck line, remove stray hair, remove hair strands on dress, adjust color and add hair on top of head, add dress on side to create better line, add dress on shoulder, clean up and smooth dress folds under arm and create one seam on image on right side. Clean up complexion, clean up neck, add blush to cheek, add highlights to earrings, add hair on top of head, add forehead to create better line, remove stray hair on neck, remove red dress at corner of neck, add dress on shoulder to sharpen and create a better line, remove stray hair on dress, and soften neck muscle a bit, and soften neck line on image on left side. TOTAL: $1,525.00

Somehow, we seem to have an insatiable appetite for the unattainable. We welcome opportunities to put someone else on a pedestal and to believe they are paragons of perfection. This phenomenon is so fantastic, so riddled with artifice and so transparent to the reasoning mind, that it might be likened to our fascination with science fiction, and even our proclivity for superstition. Maybe creating media icons for ourselves is the adult version of believing in Prince Charming and Cinderella. Whatever the origin or dynamic, the price of COMPARISON is simply too high to pay in real life, as it takes its toll in human suffering and is a very dangerous ROADBLOCK.

In order to get back into gear and move forward, we must reevaluate our relationships with others with the maturity of our adult reasoning, rather than the magical thinking of a small child. Most of us are totally blind to this self-limiting error until this COMPARISON stops us dead in our tracks and threatens our happiness. Normally, only when we are in acute personal pain do we ask, "What's wrong with this picture?" and discover the error we have made. When we identify the ROADBLOCK of COMPARISON we see that, there it is again! Apples and oranges! Our insides to their outsides! It may take the perspective of someone besides yourself to assist you in realizing that COMPARISON leads ultimately to disappointment. Only when we are open to shifting our paradigms, are we available for new truths. Only in acute crisis do we tend to show our feelings and ask for help. Then and only then, do we reconsider new ways of thinking and living.

For the sake of illustration of the utter fallacy of COMPARISON, let me share with you several behind the scenes stories about successful people and the striking contrast between their public and their private lives. Charles Darwin did very poorly in elementary school and even failed a university medical course. Albert Einstein also did quite poorly in most of his high-school courses and flunked his college entrance exams. Babe Ruth struck out 1,330 times to eventually hit 714 home runs. Louisa May Alcott was rejected by an editor and told that she would never write anything popular. Now, more than a hundred years later, the Children's Literature Association considers Little Women one of the greatest children's books of the past 200 years.

Did you know that R.H. Macy failed at business seven times before making it big with his New York department store, Macy's? Walt Disney was once fired by a newspaper editor for having "no good ideas." Of course he went on to create Mickey Mouse, Donald Duck, win over 45 Academy Awards, build the Disney Studios, Disneyland, and Disney World, and now "Disney" is an international household word.

Even Abraham Lincoln started out in the military as a captain at the beginning of the Blackhawk War. By the end of the war he had been demoted to private. Thomas Edison's teachers thought him "too stupid to learn" and he made 3,000 mistakes before succeeding in inventing the light bulb. He would finally hold 1,993 patents. Pablo Picasso struggled with studies and could barely read and write when his father pulled him out of school at age ten. His father even a hired tutor to work with him to prepare for secondary school, but the tutor finally gave up on him and quit. The great Sir Winston Churchill was at the bottom of his class in one school and failed the entrance exams to another school twice.

Beginning to get the picture? We rarely have a clue as to what's going on behind the scenes with other people, what their story line is actually like, or how they feel on the inside.

It was Anais Nin, who wrote, "There are very few human beings who receive the truth, complete, and staggering, by instant illumination. Most of us acquire it, fragment by fragment—on a small scale, by successive developments like a laborious mosaic." And none other than Helen Keller's teacher, Annie Sullivan wrote, "People seldom see the halting and painful steps by which the most insignificant success is achieved."

If we are completely honest with ourselves, we must admit that we crash into the COMPARISON ROADBLOCK on a regular basis. This ROADBLOCK is especially insidious because it is so difficult to detect and so pervasive. A therapist is privileged to see on a daily basis the true thoughts and feelings of individuals facing the challenges of COMPARISON, taking them on, determined to discover the truth. They begin the journey with feelings of being incongruent, keeping secrets, feeling inadequate, putting up a false front, and, their symptoms include depression, anxiety and stress. They invariably aspire to wholeness, truth and authenticity. They begin to feel healthier and happier when they can say to others, "What you see is what you get!" They come to therapy to identify and then remove their masks, so they can feel more connected with themselves and then, more intimate with others.

On a lighter note, sometimes through the eyes of children, we see how the process of mentoring, a functional form of role-modeling involving comparison coupled with faith, enthusiasm and optimism is not a ROADBLOCK at all, but a road sign. Children embrace their heroes and legends. They connect the dots between themselves and the ones they see as great. Children are gifted with believing the truth, that, with faith, all things are possible, and they thrive on role models and hold them in their hearts. Children are often inspired and encouraged by greatness, not diminished by defeatism.

We can learn a lot from our children. They are our teachers.

In fact, they seem to have been put in our lives to help us remove our ROADBLOCKS and begin to see the possibilities that lie ahead of us, rather than the obstacles. Even the Bible says, "Unless you become as a little child you will in no way enter into the kingdom of heaven."

I love the spirit of William Howard Taft's great-granddaughter, who, in her third grade autobiography wrote,

> *My great grandfather was President of the United States.*
> *My grandfather was a United States Senator.*
> *My father is an ambassador. And I am a Brownie!*

We know we are conquering this ROADBLOCK when we begin to live our life boldly, for the sheer joy of it, and as though we knew we could not fail. Douglas Mallock encourages us to cultivate ourselves, to appreciate who we are, rather than to attempt the impossible and outdo another at his own game:

Be the Best of Whatever You Are

> *If you can't be a pine on the top of the hill,*
> *Be a scrub in the valley, but be*
> *The best little scrub by the side of the hill*
> *Be the bush if you can't be a tree.*

> *If you can't be a bush, be a bit of the grass*
> *And some highway happier make,*
> *If you can't be a muskee, then just be a bass.*
> *But the loveliest bass in the lake!*

"C" is for COMPARISON

We can't all be captains; we've got to be crew.
There is something for all of us here.
There is big work to do, and there's lesser to do,
And the task we must do is the near.

If you can't be a highway, then just be a trail.
If you can't be the sun, be a star.
It isn't by size that you win or you fail.
Be the best of whatever you are.

 **is for KNOW-IT-ALL**

*"When we begin to take our
failures nonseriously, it means
we are ceasing to be afraid of
them. It is of immense importance
to learn to laugh at ourselves.
Angels can fly 'cause they take
themselves lightly."*

Katherine Mansfield

K is for KNOW-IT-ALL. The "K" in ROADBLOCKS stands for "KNOW-IT-ALL," a state of mind that blinds us to our shortcomings and covers our ears to new information. I am fully aware that "KNOW-IT-ALL" doesn't fit very neatly into our acronym system of ROADBLOCKS. You see, as I expose this most dreadful obstacle to our happiness and success, even I feel the knee-jerk compulsion to let you know that I'm not stupid, and to make a case for being right. So there you have embedded within the titling of this chapter, the author's exposure of the KNOW-IT-ALL ROADBLOCK. Defensiveness, perfectionism, insecurity and self-consciousness are all hallmarks of this bump in the road.

KNOW-IT-ALL is a ROADBLOCK because it leads to the most bizarre behaviors, wreaking havoc in relationships and causing us great conflict and consternation. My husband likes to tell the story that he's learned the secret of a happy marriage. Basically, it is practicing exactly the opposite of the KNOW-IT-ALL mindset. Whenever a husband and wife disagree or collide in any way on any topic whatever, the husband is to say automatically to the wife, "You're right, I'm sorry!" He and I joke about this sometimes, and he'll reply to my cheery, "Good morning!" with, "You're right, I'm sorry!" Or if I say, "Let's go to the movies," He'll answer, "You're right, I'm sorry!"

Chalk it up to personal insecurity coupled with false pride, one of the strongest motivations among us human beings is the need to be right. I once gave a talk for a large gathering entitled, "You're Right. I'm Happy!" The point is quite elemental: If we can sidestep the KNOW-IT-ALL ROADBLOCK and adopt a measure of humility, we will have a lot more fun, and a lot more friends!

The KNOW-IT-ALL ROADBLOCK brings out our talent for rationalization and justification. The KNOW-IT-ALL is capable of rearranging the very order of life itself to suit one's purposes. I'm sure it was a KNOW-IT-ALL who wrote the following verse:

Reverse Living.

Life is tough. It takes up a lot of your time and all of your weekends. And what do you get at the end of life? Death! What a reward! I think that the life cycle is all backwards. You should die first and get it out of the way. Then you live 20 years in an old age home and you get kicked out when you are too young. You get a gold watch and you go to work and you work for 40 years until you are young enough to enjoy your retirement. Then you go to college and you play and you party until you are ready for high school. And you go to high school and then you go to grade school. Then you become a little child and you have fun and you play and you have no responsibilities. And then you become a little baby and you go back into the womb. That's a real trick! You spend your last 9 months floating, and then you finish off as a gleam in somebody's eye!

Unfortunately, the KNOW-IT-ALL ROADBLOCK is particularly resistant to detection by the individual. The dilemma is evident. How does one discover one's character flaws if convinced that one is already perfect? The KNOW-IT-ALL has to be right, has an aggrandized notion of self-importance, lacks empathy for others, and is just about as defended against criticism as Fort Knox is against thieves. The KNOW-IT-ALL often suffers from narcissistic tendencies, if not the full-blown personality disorder of narcissism. Many times, these individuals have resumes, bank accounts and portfolios to support their inflated egos. Their high-rolling lifestyles and their feelings of entitlement only further fortify their false selves, the fortresses they have erected against unwanted challenges or input. Yes, the KNOW-IT-ALL ROADBLOCK is one of the most challenging, not only to recognize, but also to dismantle and clear out of our way.

Deep inside the KNOW-IT-ALL, there is inevitably an inner child of an emotional age much younger than twelve. The blustery or bombastic external façade of the KNOW-IT-ALL belies the timid and frightened emotional heart of an individual who is very insecure, very needy, and completely invested in keeping all this vulnerability a secret—even from himself!

Obviously, the KNOW-IT-ALL does not present for therapy enthusiastically, if at all. A narcissistic individual is not likely to ask for help of any kind, not even executive coaching, sports psychology, or peak performance work, without there being a major crisis at hand. It is typically their romantic relationship that has hit the wall and their family and finances that are at stake. Likewise, it is usually their partner who is in pain and about to leave them, who schedules the initial appointment. The KNOW-IT-ALL's counterpart has finally had enough of being controlled, berated, nagged or raged at and begins to stand up for herself and grow up, realizing gradually her part of the painful coupling. She (or he) usually suffers from low self-esteem, chronic self doubts, and fears losing the apparent strength and all the "magic" that the narcissistic partner seems to bring to the relationship.

A true test of the KNOW-IT-ALL's dedication to restoration of mental and emotional health is his or her willingness to establish an honest relationship with the therapist, begin to let the walls down ever so slowly, and gradually, begin to expose his own ROADBLOCK for what it really is—merely a defense mechanism erected over time to protect a frightened child.

When clients faced with this particular ROADBLOCK call me for professional services, they are usually reporting a problem, rather than presenting themselves as the problem. Their demeanor is usually very polished and controlled, while they are emphatic about the problem. Of course, they do not ascribe to the famous assertion from Pogo, "We have met the enemy and he is us." The problem is always something or someone else. For instance, "My husband has an anger problem and we need marriage counseling," or, "My boss is driving me crazy and I need career counseling and help for my stress." No matter what the "presenting problem," this prospective client is calling for professional intervention as a last resort. For individuals facing the KNOW-IT-ALL ROADBLOCK, asking for help of any kind is an especially painful and difficult step. The humility required to ask for true help usually feels like humiliation to the person with a KNOW-IT-ALL ROADBLOCK, and therefore, reaching out for assistance is practically impossible to do.

The first three steps towards greater personal power and resolution of inner conflict are so counter-intuitive for most of us that we simply stop short of taking them. For us, they feel like stepping out over a gaping crevasse with no visible means of support, much like Indiana Jones in the movie "Raiders of the Lost Ark." In recovery terms, these first three steps of the Twelve Steps are called, "the surrender steps." The very word, "surrender" is anathema to an individual faced with the KNOW-IT-ALL ROADBLOCK. Ironically, it takes a strong sense of self-confidence, based on humility, to take the three steps that allow us to remove this obstacle to greater enlightenment.

The key to removing this ROADBLOCK is found in our ability to make the following movements of consciousness:

1. *I come to believe that I am powerless over (fill in the blank), that my life is unmanageable, and that I need help.*
2. *I come to believe that there is a Higher Power that can restore me to sanity.*
3. *I make a decision to turn my life and my will over to the care of that Higher Power.*

Whether or not you are consciously working the Twelve Steps as adopted by Alcoholics Anonymous, Codependents Anonymous, or any of over four hundred variations of the Twelve Step programs, if you are committed to excellence and self-improvement, you are in the process of moving through the stages of awareness that are described not only in the Twelve Steps, but in every major spiritual movement on the planet today. At the foundation of all self-improvement is the implicit tripod of the first three steps, "surrender."

Identifying a problem that you cannot solve alone, and admitting that you need help are actually signs of strength rather than weakness. The irony in accepting our imperfections and our need for outside consultation, information, or perspective is that only those of us who can make it past the KNOW-IT-ALL stage of embarrassment or inferiority feelings, ever open the way for true greatness. When we feel too proud or frightened to take these steps, we lose. This ROADBLOCK keeps us stalled in our own misery. The mere awareness that we are not "terminally unique" in our fear of looking foolish if we ask for help, comes with a great sigh of relief.

We are all faced by the KNOW-IT-ALL mentality at various times throughout our lives, indeed, sometimes many times each day, and must move though the "surrender" steps of consciousness on a regular basis. Merely recognizing that our need to look good to others and to appear in control is a ROADBLOCK rather than a virtue is a major advance forward.

This awareness, that perfectionism is the plague of insecure and compulsive individuals rather than the badge of honor of success, usually affords one the freedom to go into overdrive in terms of personal and professional mastery. Only when we admit to the perpetual role of student that we play in life, can we open up to new information. Only then, by admitting our "weaknesses" can we be strong enough to apologize to those we may have harmed. Only then, can we ask for help from a professional, someone who can work with us in a partnership with mutual respect and what the great psychologist Dr. Carl Rogers termed, "unconditional positive regard."

Therapy often gets off to a predictable start for those of us staring at this ROADBLOCK. The KNOW-IT-ALL client presents as exceptionally articulate and well versed on the reasons for his or her problems, making an air-tight case for the fact that the real problem is someone else. I remember myself being a KNOW-IT-ALL client during a session with a therapist before starting treatment for codependency. It was late November in the snow-covered hills north of Montreal, and I was holding forth, passionately describing my problem as being about 6' 3" with silver hair and answering to the name of my husband! So convinced was I that he was my problem, that I assumed that my purpose in the consultation was to inform the therapist how she should fix him. Fortunately, I finally found myself letting the KNOW-IT-ALL guard down, as she told me gently and lovingly in her French Canadian accent, "Sweetheart, everything will be okay." I began codependency treatment within a week for being such a KNOW-IT-ALL.

Tragically, the KNOW-IT-ALL is often not even the client. Psychology and the other helping professions are literally magnets for professional codependents. Most of us are drawn into the profession to find out what's the matter with us, if not our families and friends, although we would never let this get out. There's a hidden but powerful pay-off for "helping" other people, as the "expert," of course. The therapist is actually a professional KNOW-IT-ALL when he or she is unaware of the codependency lurking beneath the motivations to "help." The pay-off for a therapist to play the role of expert, blind to his or her own "fixing disease," is simply that one does not have to look inside and fix oneself.

Just about the time I was completing my own therapy for codependency I came upon this delightful questionnaire designed to help professionals determine if their motivations are real, or codependent. Kind of like, "Is it real, or Memorex?"

1. *Do you occasionally counsel heavily after disappointment, a quarrel, or when the boss gives you a hard time?*

2. *When you have trouble or feel under pressure, do you always counsel more than usual?*

3. *Have you noticed that you are able to handle more people to counsel than you did when you were first counseling?*

4. *Did you ever wake up on the 'morning after' and discover that you could not remember part of the evening counseling, even though your friends tell you that you did not 'pass out'?*

5. *At a party, do you feel uncomfortable if there is no one there to counsel?*

6. *Do you sometimes feel a little guilty about your counseling?*

7. *Are you secretly irritated when your family or friends discuss your counseling?* ·

8. *Do you often find that you wish to continue counseling after your friends say they have had enough?*

9. *Do you usually have a reason for the occasions when you counsel heavily?*

10. *Do you often regret things you have done or said while counseling?*

11. *Have you often failed to keep the promises you have made to yourself about controlling or cutting down on your counseling?*

12. *Have you ever tried to control your counseling by making a change in jobs, moving to a new location, or going on the wagon?*

The ROADBLOCK of the KNOW-IT-ALL sometimes appears as if from out of no-where, during the course of therapy with individuals who have been moving along at quite a clip towards their stated goals. It is not at all uncommon for therapy to have a most auspicious beginning, only to hit a ROADBLOCK along the way. There are several junctures in the course of self-discovery where it is common for the client to experience what is known as the "approach-avoidance curve." By "approach-avoidance" I am referring to the natural tendency among us all to move towards our goals with motivation, and every good intention, at first. Then, gradually, as we realize that the doors to self-discovery are right around the corner, we begin to put on the brakes, sometimes slamming them on, and doing an abrupt U-turn, right out the door. We find plenty of excuses for our precipitous departure from therapy, some of the standards being, "It's too expensive," "My insurance isn't paying," "I'm too busy during the Holiday Season," "My child needs braces," or "I just need to take a break." One of my favorite excuses for backing out of therapy just as one is about to make a significant breakthrough is, "I just want to try this on my own for a while."

As things move along, and the client inevitably begins to recognize ROADBLOCKS coming into view, there is a very natural tendency to pull back, protect the unchallenged belief system that is causing one's problems, and quit. There is a moment of truth in every therapy intervention when the client realizes that the common denominator among all her problems, dilemmas, and disappointments is, in truth, herself. Really good therapy involves the client's journey into self-discovery, self-awareness and the epiphanies of seeing how it all fits together—when suddenly, finally, everything makes sense. Alexander Pope, English poet of the 18th century, encouraged such self-awareness in his famous couplet:

Know then thyself, presume not God to scan;
The proper study of mankind is man.

Therapy, counseling, even coaching involves delving into oneself, taking stock of one's past, taking inventory of one's beliefs, feelings and expectations. Whether we are an athlete facing self-imposed limitations, a public speaker overcoming stage fright, or a spouse committed to doing our part to enhance our relationship, looking inside ourselves is an integral part of our success. Introspection usually leads to identifying thoughts, beliefs, or unchallenged attitudes that have been holding us back from our goals..

Taking positive action by systematically eliminating unwanted baggage is called, "taking an inventory." Every successful business or corporation routinely takes inventory to make room for new ideas and merchandise that are more appealing, useful and profitable. Our personal inventory might be likened to a cleansing process, not unlike cleaning out a long forgotten closet full of out-dated clothing, all dusty and crowded, just taking up space.

Once again, the late, great poet Shel Silverstein provides in verse, the power of our avoidance of the inevitable in his wonderful poem, "Sarah Cynthia Sylvia Stout Would Not Take the Garbage Out":

"K" is for KNOW-IT-ALL

Sarah Cynthia Sylvia Stout
Would not take the garbage out!
She'd scour the pots and scrape the pans,
Candy the yams and spice the hams,

And though her daddy would scream and shout,
She simply would not take the garbage out.

And so it piled up to the ceilings:
Coffee grounds, potato peelings,
Brown bananas, rotten peas,
Chunks of sour cottage cheese.

It filled the can, it covered the floor,
It cracked the window and blocked the door
With bacon rinds and chicken bones,
Drippy ends of ice cream cones,

Prune pits, peach pits, orange peel,
Gloppy glumps of cold oatmeal,
Pizza crust and withered greens,
Soggy beans and tangerines,

Crusts of black burned buttered toast,
Gristly bits of beefy roasts . . .
The garbage rolled on down the hall,
It raised the roof, it broke the wall . . .

Greasy napkins, cookie crumbs,
Globs of gooey bubble gum,
Cellophane from green baloney,
Rubbery, blubbery macaroni,

Peanut butter, caked and dry,
Curdled milk and crusts of pie,

Moldy melons, dried up mustard
Eggshells mixed with lemon custard,

Cold french fries and rancid meat,
Yellow lumps of Cream of Wheat.
At last the garbage reached so high
That finally it touched the sky.

And all the neighbors moved away,
And none of her friends would come to play.
And finally Sarah Cynthia Stout said,
"OK, I'll take the garbage out!"

But then, of course, it was too late . . .
The garbage reached across the state,
From New York to the Golden Gate.
And there, in the garbage she did hate,

Poor Sarah met an awful fate,
That I cannot right now relate
Because the hour is much too late.

But children, remember Sarah Stout
And always take the garbage out!

For most of us, taking stock of our baggage, our memories and residual feelings, looking inside ourselves to the ignored recesses of our souls, our respective personal storage closets, is quite a chore. As we review our most poignant and memorable experiences, the traumas, the joys—all the "hello's and good-bye's" of our lives, we experience a flood of feelings associated with a parade of relatives, lovers, friends, and enemies, past and present. For most of us, this is a fearsome process, mostly because we revisit not only pleasant memories, but also feelings of intense sadness, anger, loss or shame that we have been denying, avoiding, or medicating for years. Taking this inventory is the required and deliberate stroll down memory lane that exposes for us the unique plot of the story line that has helped shape us into who we are today.

It is at this stage in therapy, ironically, just as we are admitting how little we know, that we are becoming what I call, "emotionally literate." We are now beginning to approach life and others as adults, realizing that our wishes and our needs are not always the same, and that disappointment, frustration and acceptance of occasional personal failures are part of adapting to life. This stage in therapy is actually a turning point in one's life. It is here that we sort out the victims from the victors, the whiners from the winners, the wimps from the wise. At this stage of exposing the ROADBLOCK of the KNOW-IT-ALL , we realize that life is indeed is a classroom, filled with lessons. We can learn them now, or we can learn them later, but for all of us, life is a required course.

Essentially, we are all learning lessons. Some of us learn more gracefully than others. Some require more pain, lower "bottoms," harder brick walls. Nonetheless, as the KNOW-IT-ALL is exposed and its defensive façade unmasked, we start to accept our role as student. When we admit that, really, we know very little, that's when the learning and the healing begin. Finally, we live life with our eyes open, and begin to understand its rules.

The Rules for Being Human

1. *You will receive a body. You may like it or hate it, but it will be yours for the entire period this time around.*

2. *You will learn lessons.* You are enrolled in a full-time informal school called life. Each day in this school you will have the opportunity to learn lessons. You may like the lessons or think them irrelevant and stupid.

3. *There are no mistakes, only lessons.* Growth is a process of trial and error experimentation. The 'failed' experiments are as much a part of the process as the experiment that ultimately 'works.'

4. *A lesson is repeated until it is learned. A lesson will be presented to you in various forms until you have learned it.* When you have learned it, you can then go on to the next lesson.

5. *Learning lessons does not end.* There is no part of life that does not contain its lessons. If you are alive, there are lessons to be learned.

6. *'There' is no better than 'here.'* When your 'there' has become a 'here,' you will simply obtain another 'there' that will, again, look better than 'here.'

7. *Others are merely mirrors of you.* You cannot love or hate something about another person unless it reflects to you something you love or hate about yourself.

8. *What you make of your life is up to you.* You have all the tools and resources you need. What you do with them is up to you. The choice is yours.

9. *Your answers lie inside you. The answers to life's questions lie inside you. All you need to do is look, listen, and trust.*

10. *You will forget all this.*

If we are successful in removing the KNOW-IT-ALL ROADBLOCK, we soon see the truth in John Lennon's quote, "Life is what happens while you're making other plans." Perhaps the best advice is to expect the unexpected, and smile!

Once we have dared look deep inside and take stock of the ghosts of past and present, we begin to recognize the fact that our inner reality, our feelings, hopes and dreams, are more like those of other people than they are different. The content, the story lines, the specifics may differ, but the process is just the same.

At the beginning of the inventory process, most of us are emotionally illiterate, or at least, emotionally dyslexic, to some degree or other. We struggle mightily with the powerful feelings that erupt as we begin to sort through the memories that have brought us here. We are faced with the obvious, that we have gotten here by trial and error, and the KNOW-IT-ALL part of us, does NOT want to admit the errors. We frequently confuse having made a mistake, with being a mistake just as we confuse guilt or regret with shame. The KNOW-IT-ALL part of us wants to forget completely about therapy after about three or four sessions. That fearful part would prefer to move along by medicating our feelings in some new and improved way, maybe with antidepressants, food or alcohol—anything to avoid taking the dreaded inventory. In a classic paradox, it is in admitting our imperfections that we begin to perfect ourselves. As we take stock of our failings, we succeed. In surrendering the KNOW-IT-ALL in ourselves, we become wise.

I find that at this point, clients experience a paradigm shift that must accompany their ascent to a higher level of consciousness, a greater awareness and deeper understanding of themselves and of others. This shift in perspective includes the undeniable fact that life is not fair, but it is how we play the hand we are dealt that we define ourselves. The following verse captures in a most poignant way, how this shift in perspective feels from the inside:

After a while you learn the subtle difference
between holding a hand and chaining a soul,
And you learn that love doesn't mean leaning and
company doesn't mean security,
And you begin to learn that kisses aren't contracts
and presents aren't promises,
And you begin to accept your defeats with your
head up and your eyes open, with the grace of an
adult, not the grief of a child.
And you learn to build all your roads on today
because tomorrow's ground is too uncertain for plans.
After a while you learn that even sunshine burns if
you get too much,
So plant your own garden and decorate your own
soul, instead of waiting for someone to bring you
flowers.
And you learn that you really can endure . . . that
you really are strong,
And you really do have worth.

 is for SUCCESS MYTHS

*"Excellence means when a
man or woman asks of himself
more than others do."*

Ortega Y Gassett

is for SUCCESS MYTHS. The ROADBLOCK of SUCCESS MYTHS comprises a false sense of what constitutes success and a misunderstanding of the process of living a successful life. Like everything else, we collect these myths piecemeal, in a fairly haphazard manner, and begin to piece them together into a kind of patchwork safety blanket that we carry well into our adult life. The child within us believes that success comes like presents from Santa on a Christmas morning, instantaneously, a miracle of abundance, right down the chimney. The older "adult child" within us also sees success in outer things, fast cars, McMansions, ivy league educations, seven digit incomes, beautiful mates, ad infinitum—in short, fortune and fame for one and all. The "just add water and stir" generation has given way to the "point and click" generation with its need for speed, ever shorter attention spans, and its demand for the lifestyles of the rich and famous. Those of us who have not harnessed the power of our own technological advances may experience its tyranny, and may find ourselves crashing into the ROADBLOCK of SUCCESS MYTHS at gigaspeed.

With the advent of the personal computer we now measure satisfaction in gigabytes, bandwidth and something called "RAM." With the information superhighway eliminating speed limits to success and promising to connect people faster, faster, faster, it's as though we are all caught up in a new millenium gold rush in which speed, not gold, is the coin of the realm. As we read our daily papers which feature the champagne and balloon celebrations of the IPO du jour gone public with its high school drop out executives now instant millionaires, our SUCCESS MYTHS leave us scratching our collective head and wondering just where we missed the boat.

Paradoxically, in this era in which we can communicate with people half a globe away in chat rooms with a click of a mouse, we are, in fact, feeling more alienated, depressed and stressed than we did when we used to chat with a neighbor over a cup of coffee or across the backyard fence. We are now crashing into the ROADBLOCK of SUCCESS MYTHS at breakneck speed, victims of our own delusions.

Our SUCCESS MYTHS feed on our own immaturity in which instant gratification is a requirement, a given. When we are caught up in this virtual race for instant fortune and fame, the feelings of entitlement to the "American Dream," the junk food mentality that prefers image over substance and stimulation over spirituality, we might be likened to the tail wagging the dog. Our appetite for excess leads to our feeling bloated, bored and, possibly even worse, baffled by life's real issues. SUCCESS MYTHS distract us from facing ourselves, looking within at the feelings and yearnings that make us human. They leave us disconnected. In the jargon of this computer age, SUCCESS MYTHS are like computer viruses. They corrupt our foundational beliefs and disable our hard drives.

SUCCESS MYTHS result from externalizing our realities, living our lives from the outside in, rather than from the inside out. When we rely on things external to ourselves to define ourselves and give our lives meaning, we are living a SUCCESS MYTH. Daily examples abound. Outside-in living includes the need to make all "A's" in school, to be the captain of the football team, to gain the approval of others, to be recognized in the community, to make a million dollars, to (fill in the blank). While aspiring to excel is intrinsic to our happiness, indeed to the survival of the species, it becomes a cancer if it supercedes one's sense of inner meaning, values and knowledge. The inevitable result of this upside-down life is spiritual bankruptcy, emotional emptiness and feelings of dejection, disillusionment and disappointment. It's the "is that all there is?" phenomenon that we feel when we've climbed the highest mountain in our lives, and, once on top, look around and wonder, "Well, if I accomplished this, it must not have been so wonderful after all!"

A classic illustration of how SUCCESS MYTHS result in despair is captured in the Greek legend of Icarus who constructed wings of wax and feathers, and then flew so high that the sun melted the wax, causing him to crash into the sea. Many of us buy into the artifice of the SUCCESS MYTHS and achieve temporary glory, only to self-destruct. When our self-image does not match our outer achievement, we doubt the legitimacy of our success, and find ways to crash and burn. As if suffering from the Icarus Complex, many of us reflexively spoil the exhilaration of our achievements, by medicating ourselves right back into our comfort zones. Over the years, I have worked with dozens and dozens of highly talented individuals who have flown high, only to over-eat, over-drink, or somehow restore themselves to feelings of mediocrity and despair. Their comfort zones might be truly miserable, and appear tragic to the rest of us, but they are home sweet home for those unable to fully own their successes and believe in themselves.

Over the years, I have worked with countless individuals whose lives had been torn apart by substance abuse. Many times these people were highly accomplished professionals, holding important positions in the community, well-known persons whose secret addictions were threatening all they had worked for in their careers, all that they cherished in personal relationships. I have seen miracles unfold in the lives of so many of these remarkable individuals who, sitting across from me in my office, by taking "the first step" of admitting they needed help and that they were powerless over their problem, spanned the chasm separating those who experience the grace of healing from those who do not.

Success is as much what you are willing to quit as what you are willing to do. Edgar A. Guest captures this challenge to success in his well-loved poem, "True Grit":

How much grit do you think you got?
Can you quit a thing that you like a lot?
You may talk of spunk,
It's an easy word,
And where ere you go
It is often heard
But can you tell—
Or care to guess
Just how much courage you possess?

How much grit do you
Think you got?
Can you turn from joys
That you like a lot?

Have you ever tested yourself to know
How far with yourself your will will go?

If you want to know if
You have grit,
Just pick out a joy you like
And quit!

Often the greatest success is the simplest and most silent movement of the heart. The tiny, yet monumental act of surrender distinguishes those who ultimately succeed from those who fail. The paradox at play here is that, in the realm of success, greatness and wonder, it is in "surrendering" one's will, one's own way to that of a Higher Power, and then being willing to go to any lengths to implement the required changes—that separates the victims from the victorious, the struggling from the successful.

Each of us carries within our hearts a few treasured and precious memories of the taste of excellence, moments when we touched the stars for even a brief moment and felt the exhilaration of becoming more than we dared even hope we could be. For most of us, these often secret, but shining moments in the sun are held close within our hearts. They are our symbols of success, no matter how long ago and far away they might seem to others. To us, they will always remain our defining moments, a source of pride and hope for moments of transcendence and overcoming yet to be.

These personal treasures that each of us carry as we move about our daily lives remind me of the contents of the tiny wooden box that the Charles Tazewell's timeless masterpiece The Littlest Angel retrieved from underneath his bed on Earth and took to heaven to show to the Understanding Angel. Our individual collection of memories may appear to be as humble as the "sky-blue egg from a bird's nest in the olive tree that stood to shade his mother's kitchen door" or as tattered as the "limp, tooth-marked leather strap, once worn as a collar by his mongrel dog, who had died as he had lived, in absolute love and infinite devotion."

Our SUCCESS MYTHS would have us compare our offerings to Heaven, the contents of our own "small, rough, unsightly box," with those of presidents and kings, CEO's and illustrious stars of stage and screen, persons we may deem better than ourselves. And, like the Littlest Angel, most of us shrink in shame, feeling that instead of honoring God with our personal best, we have instead "been most blasphemous." When faced head on with the ROADBLOCK of SUCCESS MYTHS, we feel utterly lacking and unworthy, no matter how high we climb and how brightly we shine—we're still never quite good enough.

I meet daily with clients who have fallen off the top of the class, the earning curve or the corporate ladder. They are sometimes in their twenties or thirties when they crash into the ceiling of their aspirations and come to talk with me about what could possibly be wrong with this picture. Usually these are the most talented and affable of people, not what you might see on reruns of the "Bob Newhart Show," yet they are seeking professional help to address the vague, nameless sense within themselves that something is dreadfully wrong.

Fortunately, for most, they eventually recognize the fallacy of trying to succeed by living from the outside in. They see that while they've been nurturing their external dreams and measuring their progress by grades, positions or bank accounts, they have been doing so at the expense of their inner lives. They have been letting their inner identities atrophy and perish, while they've been force-feeding their egos. They report feeling off balance, dissatisfied and quite frequently they present with symptoms of substance abuse, overspending, marital problems or legal woes. As they began to wither inside from a lack of spiritual nourishment, most began self-medicating to numb the pain and to substitute the fleeting pleasure of spending, eating, drinking, or "sexing" for the happiness which eludes them.

The SUCCESS MYTHS in their lives had seduced them from life's true treasures, and now, only after crashing into this ROADBLOCK, do these travelers down life's highway begin the process of making a paradigm shift to live from the inside out. For most, this is like learning to walk all over again, or learning to change from being right-handed to using one's left hand. The shift in perspective is so radical and requires such vigilance to maintain that, I've been told many times, "It just doesn't feel right," and "It feels scary," or "I am too impatient to do it that way." I've seen men and women from their teens to their seventies sitting in class at treatment centers, literally going back to school to learn how to live. I've seen young and old alike sitting at desks, taking stock of their lives in inventories which helped them trace their way back to a time when life made sense and then, step by step, re-charting a path for a truly successful life, from the inside out.

A very common example of a SUCCESS MYTH is the delusional reasoning by a person who stays in a marriage that died years ago. This living with a dead marriage is like propping up a corpse in the living room and pretending to make conversation with it—it's crazy! When one is living this lie, the SUCCESS MYTH reasoning goes like this: "Well, it is very important to stay married, because if I were to divorce I would have failed." Or, sometimes the excuse is more like, "I need to stay married to maintain stability for the family," or, "I need to stay in the marriage for security's sake." Any way you slice it, the SUCCESS MYTH for persons stuck in this quagmire of relationship inertia seems to be a rationale for the status quo and a prescription for failure.

Clearly when we are faced with the SUCCESS MYTH, just as with any other ROADBLOCK, we sometimes mistake it for a perfectly good parking place and simply run our engines in idle, going nowhere, but appeasing ourselves with the notion that this is what we're supposed to do, this is where we're supposed to be, somewhere in the great parking lot of life. Quite remarkably, with this awareness that it is not the parking space per se that must be maintained, but rather one's own personal and spiritual development, then and only then is one capable of giving one's attention to repairing the true problem, and that, of course is the status quo within ourselves, the static and stagnant personal qualities that have gone unexamined and unperfected.

Ironically, it is within relationships that we are the most likely to view ourselves, the good, the bad and the ugly, and thereby attend to improving our character flaws and our personal shortcomings. Relationships serve as mirrors for us to see ourselves as others see us, and then, faced with the truth, take stock of ourselves and sort out what is welcome and what is ready for the trash heap.

In relationship counseling, I have seen thousands of couples shift their focus from the problem with their partners to the problems within themselves, and with that sheer shift of attention and intention, begin to heal and develop their relationship. In fact, it is often the most "hopeless" of relationships that eventually heals and exceeds all expectations with new levels of mutual support and satisfaction, respect and renewed enthusiasm.

Like every ROADBLOCK, that of the SUCCESS MYTH catches us off guard, comes up quickly to block our way, and has no neon sign flashing "BEWARE OF ROADBLOCKS." Also, similar to each and every other ROADBLOCK, the SUCCESS MYTH is almost always a disguise for some of our character flaws, our shortcomings.

In the instance of the individual parked in a dead marriage, the ROADBLOCK distracts us from the fact that we are afraid of the unknown, afraid of being on our own, worried about others' reactions and admonitions if we were to leave, terrified of confrontation and, ultimately, feeling about five years old and about to be marched down to the principal's office. The SUCCESS MYTH serves the purpose of protecting us from having to face our fears. We can use it as a "noble" reason to avoid what frightens us and thereby to shrink from our potential. For the immature, any ROADBLOCK will do to forestall the unknown, to avoid life and to stay "safely" stalled.

It takes a while to mature. We all learn lessons the hard way. Usually we have to create a problem in order to learn life's lessons. With time and patience we finally recognize the need to remove all our ROADBLOCKS, including that of the SUCCESS MYTHS in order to clear our way to experience meaning, fulfillment and true happiness. It is the mature adult within us who sets out to gain a deeper understanding of what success really means. This mature adult puts aside childish, worn-out beliefs about success, just as he or she puts away worn-out clothing, and starts fresh, with an open mind, sorting out the counterfeit glitter from the genuine treasure. In the words of George Herbert Parker, "The most consummately beautiful thing in the universe is the rightly fashioned life of a good person."

Ralph Waldo Emerson defined success in these oft-quoted words:

> *To laugh often and much; to win the respect of*
> *intelligent people and affection of children; to earn*
> *the appreciation of honest critics and endure the*
> *betrayal of false friends; to appreciate beauty,*

to find the best in others; to leave the world a bit
better, whether by a healthy child, a garden patch
or a redeemed social condition; to know even one
life has breathed easier because you have lived.
This is to have succeeded.

Several years ago my mother suffered a major debilitating and paralyzing stroke. As a family, for months and months we were reeling from the shock and the pain of such a blow to our loved one. Suddenly, this remarkable and wonderful woman who had been the "heart" of our family, who had given generously of her time and energies to us children, the neighbors, the community, had almost died, and was left partially paralyzed. For a year we worked with her as she progressed from intensive care, to a residential hospital rehabilitation setting, and finally back home, where her bedroom became her living room. My mother's life had been forever changed, and to all of us, it seemed tragic every time we saw her, sad beyond words for the longest time, no matter how we reminded ourselves that all things happen for a reason.

Shortly following her stoke, my mother showed me she still had plenty of hope about her future. She said, "You know, miracles are all around us. They don't appear in a flash, like a lightning bolt, with lots of noise and fanfare. They are more like twinkle lights. You notice them in little things, daily things. Miracles are everywhere."

My mother has always been a success, showing us the way, through her quiet encouragement and faith, her bold actions and her unfailing sense of humor. The following verse by Margaret Bailey entitled, "Prayer" captures the way my mother has lived:

God, give me sympathy and sense
And help me keep my courage high.
God, give me calm and confidence
And, please—a twinkle in my eye.

Since that time ten years ago, my mother is still with us and approaching her eightieth birthday. Mobilized by her faith and her determination to heal, to do new things everyday, to be a daily part of her children's and grandchildren's lives, she is learning computer skills, getting online, joining an investment club, managing all her own rent houses from her home office and always sharing a joke of the day with us. She inspires us with her enthusiasm, her indefatigable curiosity about life and her sheer vitality that transcends physical abilities. Partial physical paralysis may have been the cruel result of a stroke, but my mother demonstrates and teaches all who meet her that there is no paralysis of the spirit, without one's consent. While her physical body has slowed, my mother's spirit has soared.

Of course, opportunities disguised as disaster strike not only the person who suffers a physical disability, a serious illness or a life-threatening accident, but also the people who love them. My mother's stroke came like a lightning bolt out of the blue and left my father with a life forever altered as well. My father has always been considered to be successful. A retired Air Force Colonel, a former fighter pilot and Base Commander of Randolph Air Force Base, the "Show Place of the Air Force," my father was competitive, talented, intelligent, well respected and widely revered by all who knew him. He was a veteran of World War II whose plane was shot out of the sky over France. Seriously burned, he was captured by the Germans and held as a prisoner of war, while my mother and the rest of his family received telegrams from the U.S. War Department that he was missing in action and presumed dead. Not until Christmas Eve, 1945, did they receive a follow up telegram that he was alive and being held as a prisoner of war. What a Christmas present! Success during that era had "survival" written all over it. Real success for veterans of World War II, as for veterans of any war, was not measured so much by receiving the Purple Heart, the Medal of Honor or any such public acknowledgement of courage and bravery, as by the Grace that brought each surviving veteran home to loved ones and a grateful nation.

My father went on to have a brilliant career, raise a family of four daughters, all professionals, all with advanced graduate degrees. My father was a Rotarian, a bank vice-president, and a good neighbor. There is no doubt that my father was considered to be "successful" prior to the bolt from the blue that changed, not only my mother's life, but also my father's life, forever.

The family medical emergency of my mother's stroke transformed this invincible fighter pilot into a caretaker. This military giant in our eyes had always been given to quick decisions, keen analysis and sometimes biting but incisive criticism. He was a man of action and few words. His mettle had been tested in the embattled skies over Europe and on the ground in the German P.O.W. camps. But with my mother's stroke, my father's character, endurance and emotional stability would be tested as never before.

For more than ten years now we have watched my father become more gentle, patient, kind and understanding than we might ever have dreamed possible. Now we watch as he carefully prepares meals for my mother, takes her to the Dairy Queen for frozen custard, does all the errands, runs the household in ways that before only my mother could have done. He became the hands and feet of the family, the driver, and the grocery shopper. A decade of selfless service has actually made a truly great man out of an already successful one.

In the case of my father, all his career and family success heretofore seemed to have been blessings from above, but over the past ten years, I believe that my father has given back in ways none of us could have predicted. Louis Nizer captures this transformation beautifully in his words,

> *What we are is God's gift to us.*
> *What we become is our gift to God.*

Success seems to have more to it than starring in a role in life, excelling in a sport or sparkling on a stage. Success seems to have evolutionary qualities about it, in which we are transformed, altered, metamorphosed. I'll never forget the sunny afternoons a few years ago when I worked in my private practice with a little nine year-old girl we'll call "Molly." Molly had been referred for counseling to help her with her self-esteem. She had recently relocated to our area and was having "growing pains" when it came to making new friends and missing old ones. One day, I gave Molly some paper and a pencil and asked her if she wanted to write about how she was feeling. This is what she wrote:

Growing

Horses grow only in size,
Caterpillars change into butterflies.
We're all so different,
I don't know why.
I can't believe that birds can fly!

We have one thing in common,
That I know;
That is that we grow, and grow, and grow.

This young girl understood that life and success involve change. She was living into it and poetically expressing her wonder at how it feels to be turning inside out, transforming and growing. Through the eyes of a child, we see that success requires that we let go of the outcome and allow ourselves to be transformed.

Another young person we'll call "Annie" came to me in her early teens and suffered from severe depression. She was failing in school, unable to attend anymore, talking about suicide, and finally hospitalized. Annie's parents were beside themselves, not knowing how to help her or what to do in this very painful and serious situation. I worked with Annie throughout her hospitalization and beyond, as an outpatient. Each visit was a challenge, as Annie frequently would not have a word to say to me. Sometimes we would just meet together and I would do the visiting, allowing her to be silent. Sometimes, she and I would just sit quietly together, allowing her mood to determine the day's events.

One afternoon I shared with Annie a therapy tool that I use called, "The Image Book" in which I keep pictures and words that portray the dreams, aspirations, and personal qualities I am cultivating, in short, a book of possibilities that create an opening for new behaviors, positive changes, even miracles.

This tool is often used in occupational therapy and holds great appeal for those suffering from depression. They often feel that they are in a deep, dark hole, with no way out and no one who could ever understand or reach them. The Image Book often serves as a way out through fantasy and whatever tiny hope they have.

One day, after weeks of virtual silence and apparent stagnation in our therapy, Annie arrived at my office with a slight smile, carrying a brightly colored Image Book page she had constructed to show me. In letters cut from magazines, she had pieced together and pasted onto red construction paper the following words:

> *I believe in the sun even when it is not shining,*
> *I believe in love even when I do not feel it,*
> *And, I believe in God even when he is silent.*

As I hold that fading page in my lap now, while typing this, her faith in things unseen still brings tears to my eyes. Annie had escaped the darkness of depression through the magic of her imagination. She had succeeded through her faith.

There is, perhaps, no one more inspiring to us all in her ability to appreciate life and to "see" all the beauty of the earth than Helen Keller. To me she exemplifies true success. She writes, "Join the great company of those who make the barren places of life fruitful with kindness. Carry a vision of heaven in your hearts, and you shall make your name, your college, the world correspond to that vision. Your success and happiness lie within you. External conditions are the accidents of life, its outer wrappings. The great enduring realities are love and service. Joy is the holy fire that keeps our purpose warm and our intelligence aglow. Resolve to keep happy, and your joy and you shall form an invincible host against difficulty."

She also considers "success" in her writing, "I long to accomplish a great and noble task, but it is my chief duty to accomplish humble tasks as though they were great and noble. The world is moved along, not only by the mighty shoves of its heroes, but also by the aggregate of the tiny pushes of each honest worker."

Several years ago I had the privilege of working with a client who came to me with the emotional problems associated with a closed head injury. She was in her late twenties and her injury had left her with a severe limp, a speech impediment and some serious neurological problems, making it difficult to hold a job, drive a car or in any "normal" way, get on with her life. I remember that we worked together to coordinate her transportation to her weekly appointments, as she had to rely on others to drive her. Nonetheless, against all odds, the client whom we shall call "Cindy" faithfully arrived on time for each meeting and poured herself wholeheartedly into each session. At the start of each session she would reach into her purse to retrieve a small, spiral notebook that she referred to as, "my memory." She relied on her notes to recall the thoughts she had had that week and took notes during the session in order to remember our day's work.

Together we developed some techniques to assist her with her impaired memory; we dealt with her frustration at feeling powerless over her temper flaring or her tears flowing. Adjusting to all the overwhelming was truly daunting, and I can remember experiencing such intense personal feelings of empathy and inadequacy that I questioned whether I was of any help to her at all.

Ultimately, on the occasion of Cindy's last appointment, it was she who was my teacher about the meaning of true success. Cindy arrived at my office wearing a big smile and bearing gifts. In her limited and halting speech she thanked me for my help over the months, and then, gave me two presents. First she presented me with a needlepoint ornamental plaque, which she had designed. It said simply, "JOY" and was embellished by a small red heart. She had painstakingly crafted this herself as a Christmas gift to me, and it had taken her months to accomplish. Secondly, Cindy gave me a gift-wrapped wooden wall plaque with the following poem:

The Weaver

My life is but a weaving
Between my Lord and me.
I cannot choose the colors
He worketh steadily.

Ofttimes he weaveth sorrow,
And I in foolish pride
Forget He sees the upper
And I the underside.

Not till the loom is silent
And the shuttles cease to fly,
Shall God unroll the canvas
And explain the reason why.

The dark threads are as needful
In the Weaver's skillful hand,
As the threads of gold and silver
In the pattern He has planned.

All the while, Cindy had been my therapist. The student had been the teacher. She taught me about true success. With humility and sincerity she arrived each week, with her "memory" tucked inside her purse. Her goal was to improve her life, to learn to cope with her surging emotions, which had been altered by her injury. She made friends with my staff. She valued our relationship, and to this day, she holds a place in my heart. She set an example for me of the beauty of a simple soul striving to be its best. She showed me the truth in Booker T. Washington's statement: "Success is to be measured not so much by the position that one has reached in life as by the obstacles which he has overcome while trying to succeed."

Sometimes the road to our fulfillment is blocked by our ROADBLOCKS of SUCCESS MYTHS and part of our struggle is our belief that we must be in charge, in control and do everything ourselves. In our confusion and ignorance, we try to reinvent ourselves by ourselves! Since it is true, that one can never solve a problem from the level of the problem, our efforts are futile, and we continue to " play God" and force our future, figure out our problems and, of course, finally fail. Our western culture reinforces the fantasy of the rugged individualist and the "self made man," thereby fueling the self-destructive fires of our belief that our successes are somehow reflective of our own greatness, that we ourselves should take credit for our accomplishments and for the heights we reach.

This very book has been a tool of transformation for me and has allowed me to expose my own SUCCESS MYTHS as never before. As a child, I had imagined success in a myriad of childish ways: becoming a famous singer or actress, then later, maybe an accomplished and famous speaker and author—all the while envisioning the accomplishments as personal reflections of my own talent, persistence, character, in a most childlike and egocentric manner. Remember, we carry within us these vestigial beliefs that are just about as useful as our appendix is to our digestive tract! Claiming one's achievements in life as reflections of one's own greatness is a prime example—shortsighted and self-serving—an example of false pride than is ripe for an upgrade to humility more fitting the soul of the spiritually mature than the ego of a child.

Through dozens of incarnations of this manuscript on my word processor I have also processed literally thousands of my own relationships. I have relived moments of joy, synchronicity and wonder as well as regrets for missed opportunities to express my gratitude to a sea of humanity that has kept me afloat during times of personal failings, struggles and despair. This book, initially begun as a personal goal, a symbol of personal career success, has instead become a teacher of humility and an offering of gratitude for the sacrifices of untold and often unknown others who, by laying down their lives, their own dreams and wishes, have afforded me a forum for expression. I am humbled by their simple greatness and inspired by their generosity and selflessness. Just as in the old country saying, "When you find a turtle on a fencepost, you can bet your boots he didn't get there on his own!"

It is easy to shatter the ROADBLOCK of SUCCESS MYTHS with the consciousness that we are all connected in spirit, we need one another, and we never walk alone:

Footprints in the Sand

One night a man had a dream.
He dreamed he was walking along the beach with
the Lord.
Across the sky flashed scenes from his life.
For each scene, he noticed two sets of footprints in
the sand;
one belonging to him, and the other to the Lord.

When the last scene of his life flashed before him,
he looked back at the footprints in the sand.
He noticed that many times along the path of his
life, there was only one set of footprints.
He also noticed that it happened at the very lowest
and saddest times in his life.

This really bothered him and he questioned the
Lord about it.
'Lord, you said that once I decided to follow you,
you'd walk with me all the way.
But I have noticed that during the most troublesome
times
in my life there is only one set of footprints.
I don't understand why, when I needed you most,
you would leave me.'

The Lord replied, 'My precious, precious child,
I love you and I would never leave you.
During your times of trial and suffering, when you
see only one set of footprints in the sand, it was
then that I carried you.'

Actual success in living is accompanied by the awareness that there are ROADBLOCKS in the road of life for everyone. We come to realize that "charmed lives" exist only in fairy tales, and that each of us needs help now and then. Looking back, we recognize that it is often in times of personal pain, frustration and despair that we grow the most. To all of you who have read this book to gain self-awareness and to meet your challenges with faith and courage, I salute you. Through your faith in the power of the human spirit you will continue to face and recognize your own ROADBLOCKS and through this simple awareness, you will allow them to transform you into the person you always dreamed you could be.

EPILOGUE

I am writing this on a windy, wintry day at dawn while the holiday lights twinkle on the trees outside my study window. Cardinals, blue jays and sparrows gather on my windowsill to feast on piles of sunflower seeds I have put out for them. It's a day like any other, just hours before I go to the office to meet with clients, each engaged in their own personal pilgrimage towards their own individual points of truth.

In the department store last night as I completed my Christmas shopping, I passed by a giant digital clock which ticked off in tenths of seconds the final twelve days of the year. This enormous display of red numbers was mounted inside a store near the entrance of the mall just between the ladies' dress department and housewares. I couldn't help but feel the strange sensation of the awesome mixed with the ordinary as I passed by. A small group of shoppers joked about the backward stream of red numbers, the countdown to the New Year, as they tried to capture a tenth of a second within a sentence. It was as though we were viewing a digitized hourglass as the final grains of sand fell into a giant heap below leaving behind nothingness.

Times like this force us to face our own mortality, the question of our purpose, the meaning of our lives. Yet, just like last night in the mall, we pause to consider questions of such magnitude in the fleeting moments between making our purchases, considering our credit card limits and rummaging through our pockets or purses for the keys to our car. The moments I spent as I passed by the giant digitized symbol of my own mortality were very brief. In fact, as I look back, I remember thinking, "What a nice touch!" as I appreciated the display more as a marketing tool for the mall than for any metaphysical meaning. Now, the next morning, it appears to me that life is like that New Year's clock or the hourglass— a constant stream of curiosities. And each of us is faced daily with the task of assigning value and meaning to the ordinary, mundane things that happen to us. Sometimes we choose to fall asleep to the bigger picture. Once in a while, we step back, look up and let ourselves be overwhelmed by the mystery of it all.

Perhaps it is true that when faced with the truly profound questions about our lives, we tend to retreat into ritualistic patterns that serve as hiding places to protect ourselves from the awesome awareness of our own spiritual development. It's as if we break off bite-sized pieces of the meaning for our daily lives so that we have might have a shot at wrapping our minds around them. We shield ourselves from the magnificence of reality with calendars and commercialism, and we create holidays, anniversaries and birthdays. Within the comfort of these celebratory social constructs, we enjoy memorializing life's grandeur, all the while "dumbing" it down to something we can comprehend. It's like we realize that we have neither the patience nor the aptitude to comprehend life's classics and masterpieces, so we satisfy ourselves with the "Cliff Notes" of our existence. It's like gazing at a solar eclipse through special dark glasses or viewing only the shadow it casts through a pinhole in a piece of cardboard. To view our source directly would be blinding, and so we ponder the beauty of the season in the flickering fires of our fireplaces, in the Holiday lights on the tree and in exchange of gifts, our seasonal symbols of human kindness.

The ROADBLOCKS we face comprise an endless array of misunderstandings, frustrations, distortions of reality and feelings of futility and abandonment. When we are faced with ROADBLOCKS it is as if we are lost on a highway with no roadmap, stranded with no roadside service from "Triple A," or "On Star" global positioning system. Yet life is indeed what is happening while we are making other plans! And life's ROADBLOCKS are the nautilus machines of our very souls, through which we develop and perfect ourselves by redundant and seemingly endless lessons—repetitious, sometimes tedious, but always fruitful. Each of us is capable of recounting our own personal series of ROADBLOCKS, both past and present, with renewed awareness of the lessons learned from each. For me, it is a great personal relief to revisit the scrapbook of my youth and to dismiss as naïve and melodramatic the futility I felt at nineteen in my poetic self-portrait:

> A reverent fool whose hymns are heresy;
> A mouthpiece mute in God's ventriloquy.

Looking back now, this tortured self-image reminds me of the bad hair days of my youth, quite devastating and self-limiting at the time, but in the bigger picture, more a reflection of self-absorption and insecurity than of reality and actual potential. Within that tiny couplet, lie a number of different ROADBLOCKS. Each ROADBLOCK held the paradox of personal potential hidden by a sense of powerlessness. From each insecurity came an instinctive acceptance of new challenges, growth opportunities and goals. Just like you, I am spurred on by the awareness that I have a lot of developing to do. Even within feelings of failure there lies fuel for success. Just like you, I am driven forward to new adventures and opportunities. I am grateful that among them has been a career through which I have been privileged to help and be helped by others.

I hope that as you contemplate your own path and the

obstacles you face both now and in the future, that you will find the concept of "ROADBLOCKS" a simple and useful tool. I also hope that you will take heart and inspiration from the people whose personal disclosures help us discover that we all have far more in common than we have to separate us. No matter what your particular ROADBLOCKS might be today, you are far from being alone. No matter how frightened or isolated you might feel, help is never far away. No matter what your personal destination, you share a journey with millions, indeed, billions of others. And no matter how concerned you might be that you are out of step or out of place, remember the inspired and timeless words of Max Ehrmann's "Desiderata":

> *Beyond a wholesome discipline, be gentle with yourself. You are a child of the universe, no less than the trees and the stars; you have a right to be here. And whether or not it is clear to you, no doubt the universe is unfolding as it should.*

BON VOYAGE!

AN INVITATION TO THE READER

As you can so clearly see, REMOVING YOUR ROADBLOCKS is a book that was actually written by thousands of individuals, each striving to solve their problems and achieve their dreams.

If you have a story that you would like to share to be included in the sequel to ROADBLOCKS, please send it to me via email at jfm@mustin.com. Of course, all references to individuals will be anonymous to ensure confidentiality, just as they have been in ROADBLOCKS.

If you would like more information about my private practice of psychology or if you are interested in scheduling a speaking engagement for your company or group, please visit my Web site, www.mustin.com.

REMOVING YOUR ROADBLOCKS